AFTER LOSS

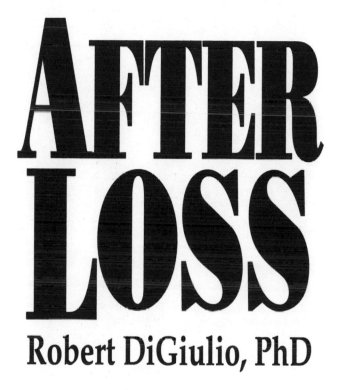

AFTER LOSS

Robert DiGiulio, PhD

WRS PUBLISHING

A Division of WRS Group, Inc.
Waco, Texas

First published in the United States of America in 1993 by WRS Publishing,
A Division of WRS Group, Inc., 701 N. New Road, Waco, Texas 76710
Book design by Kenneth Turbeville
Jacket design by Joe James

10 9 8 7 6 5 4 3 2 1

Library of Congress Catalog Card Number
DiGiulio, Robert C.

ISBN 1-56796-022-7

DEDICATION

To Emily

INTRODUCTION

In 1980 I was, in gambler's parlance, "on a roll." My two books on parenting—a hard cover and a paperback original—were published. Less than a month after its release I was thrilled to learn that my hard cover was going into its second printing. In April, my paperback publisher flew me across the United States to record a series of spoken tapes, *Robert DiGiulio Talks to Single Parents*. Marketing plans for my hard cover were being unveiled: A large budget had been earmarked by the publisher for the promotional tour, which promised my first stab at the talk-show circuit. In June and July, radio spots in Hartford, Connecticut, and Albany, New York, had been scheduled. August promised an appearance on Boston's popular "Good Day" television show. This was to be followed by three radio talk shows in upstate New York and Massachusetts, plus the obligatory author's book-signing parties at bookstores. Johnny Carson would just have to get in line and wait!

But 1980 eventually brought calamity to my family. On the day I was to receive my confirmed book-promotion itinerary, my wife, Chrissie, and our six-year-old daughter, Christine, were killed when their car was struck by a truck on a Vermont highway. Both of my wife's parents also died in that crash. From the heady joy of just having had my first two books published early in the year, my life turned sorrowful and deeply painful. The first six months brought numbness and deep distress. It was a phase spent in denial, asking many questions over and again that had no answers—at least no satisfactory answers. The first phase also brought tormented concern for the well-being of my two surviving daughters, Katie, who was just two when her mother died, and Aimee, who had turned five the day before the accident.

The second phase of my "widowerhood" was more painful—a "roller coaster." Emotions ranged from anger one moment to peace and almost well-being the next, with a sudden return to depression, and up again. One day I would feel joyful watching Aimee and Katie playing outside, happy being with each other. But later that evening I'd crash, the joy turned to intense pain from missing Chrissie and what our life had been. When the house was perfectly still (worst on Sunday nights), I even contemplated suicide in the emptiness. One evening after putting the girls to bed, Katie's simple cry for a glass of water pulled me out of it.

The second and third years were pivotal: the most painful times were behind me as I entered the third stage, "emergence." My new identity as a not-married adult started taking shape. Like a stone polished by the wind, my sharp edges were gone. I saw myself less as a pitiful survivor and more as a healing, full person—a different person. I returned to college. I began a research project and spent two years interviewing hundreds of widowed persons in the United States and Canada. Perhaps my real, underlying motive was personal. Finding out what had happened to each of them would shed light upon what had happened to *me*.

Through those years I kept a journal, making entries sometimes every day, and sometimes not for weeks. I wrote for therapy; I wrote when I needed to lay thoughts out to gain perspective, when I wanted to get my mind off things, or when I wanted to remember an event or moment. Over time my professional activity picked up as well: In 1986 a friend and I began a counseling service, and in 1987, I wrote a booklet called *Losing Someone Close*, which has now sold over 250,000 copies. Two years later, my book *Beyond Widowhood* was published. It was written for widowed persons and for the care-givers who help them.

Late in 1989 I was invited to an author's reception at the Widowed Persons Service Conference in Minneapolis. As I signed copies of my book and talked with the attendees, a beaming older woman placed her hand on mine:

"Dr. DiGiulio, I loved your book *Beyond Widowhood*—I really enjoyed it." I thanked her.

"I especially liked the part about your personal experiences—where you told about your feelings—all the personal sort of stuff on how you coped."

I told her it was an excerpt from my journal.

"But that was the best part of your book," she said. "How about writing another book? This time why not publish all of that journal?"

Thinking how personal it was, I said, "No, I don't think so," adding, "But if I ever do, it will have to be published posthumously!"

She quickly responded, "Well, good. I hope it comes out soon!"

I finally took her advice. People are not always interested in the facts, figures, and statistics of bereavement, nor in the deeply philosophical implications of death. People want to hear what helped someone (me) to survive, not because what I did was so momentous, but because it was authentic, and so is useful to them. Whether their pain is from losing a loved one or from divorce or another loss, people can better understand what they are going through when they can make connections between their experiences and those of someone who has traveled a similar path. They can also make connections between the challenges my children faced in dealing with loss and the challenges their children—all children—face.

I originally called this book *Three Years to Life*, because at first, the loss of my wife and daughter felt like a prison sentence. Like millions of hurting men and women, I often felt lonely and sad—and usually isolated, indignant, angry, vengeful, and remorseful. In scary moments, I thought about suicide. Bereavement is at first a deeply painful place to be.

Three years was a landmark of sorts, because once past that point my life seemed to be, once again, *my* life. And my life was good. That is why I changed the name to *After Loss*. For losing a loved one (or experiencing any loss ranging from divorce to retirement) is not the end of your life, nor does it mean that from now on sorrow is the dominant emotion. Regardless of its cause, a period of loss is meant to be lived through and meant to be worn out, like a set of tires on your car. When it has served its purpose, it is to be discarded. In fact, loss—your loss, any human loss—is the only springboard from which a life can take on new meaning. A new direction becomes visible, and a new happiness becomes attainable. This is not simply positive self-talk: My life is good not because of my *telling myself it is so*, but *because I have made it that way*. Not perfect, but satisfactory, not consummate, but full. There is life again after loss, and it can be a happy life, even if—especially if—it was not happy before the loss.

Early on I was fortunate. Like many other grief-stricken men and women, I had supportive friends and family with whom I could talk... about the pain, the injustice, and all else. You cannot survive loss without the support of at least one good friend.

To survive loss is, of course, the immediate goal, regardless of whom or what you have lost. But to move beyond loss and re-create a new life for yourself requires something more than survival. In the third year of bereavement I met a friend who turned out to be a special friend. I talked; we talked. When she listened, she heard not the Bob I had been but the new, changed person I had become. By doing so she helped me see—and even start to get to like—that new person I had become. So I dedicate this book to her, because she helped put the finishing touches to my hope that I would live once again.

PART ONE: EARLY ON

And what is so rare as a day in June?
Then, if ever, come perfect days;
Then Heaven tries earth if it be in tune,
And over it softly her warm ear lays...
—James Russell Lowell

1980

Brutal heat. The freak heat wave that ravaged Texas early in June worked its way north; it was in the high 80s when I awoke just before eight. (Air hot and clammy; unusual for a Vermont morning.) Went down for coffee and turned on the 8:00 a.m. news. At federal subsidy, President Jimmy Carter was offering southerners low-cost fans. News about the hostages and Ayatollah Khoumeini. Analysis of Ted Kennedy's beating Carter in New Jersey and California primaries.

My tennis lesson in Woodstock this morning; contemplated backing out due to the heat.

I thought about my book *Effective Parenting*; I would hear about the promotional plans today. *Today*. I was very up; I wanted to stay home and sit by the phone.

At 8:30 a.m. Chrissie came downstairs; I met her at the bottom step. She encouraged me to play tennis; she'd probably take the girls swimming at Stoughton Pond. She wore her favorite, faded-blue flannel nightgown.

"Do you want breakfast?" she asked.

"No thanks. I had some coffee," I replied as I stood to kiss her. She pulled away, teasing in mock shame.

"Noo! I have draa-gon mouth!" she laughed, mimicking a television mouthwash commercial portrayal of those poor souls who did not use their brand of mouthwash-plus-breath freshener.

I called "Bye, everybody!" to my mother-in-law, Olga, and daughter Christine, who were snuggled on the sofa bed off in the other room. Everyone else was still asleep upstairs, unwilling, I guess, to face the heat.

Chrissie smiled at me as I walked out the door; she was on the porch as I got in my white VW Rabbit. She called out the time-tested phrase of couples married for ten or more years:

"What would you like for supper?"

"Someplace air-conditioned!" I answered.

She winked and smiled. Someone called "MAAAAAA!" from within the house. She rolled her eyes.

I started the car, waved to her, and I never saw her again.

My car is somewhere in Woodstock; I am at Springfield Hospital. A Vermont state trooper brings me in; I sit somewhere; people dressed in white give me water and pills. They tell me to take them. They give me more. I sit down; I stand up; I start to run away. Someone runs after me. I recognize him—my friend John. "John, was it a big truck that hit them? Are they lying to me, John? John, where are my children? You know Aimee and Katie. John, they said my Christine died."

A doctor says something to me. I can't hear anything. Is it true? He took my hand and walked me somewhere. A nurse's station. I tell a tall man behind it who I am and I want my children. When he hears my name he looks pained, points to a room across the way.

Katie. *Katie.* She is in a clear plastic crib; part of her head is shaved. A spot of blood.

I pick her up. She sees who I am. She says "Dada" and clings tightly to me. I will *never* let her out of my arms again. Someone keeps telling me Aimee is alive, too, and she will be here with me soon. I can't stand up even though I try. Katie's little body has purple welts making a clear "V" from shoulder to abdomen to shoulder. Her cheek is bandaged, as is her right arm. Is it broken? Someone says no, it's only scratched. From glass. She is alive. All right. I won't let go of her; I sit on a cot with her against my chest. It's my fault because I let go of them. I won't let go again.

The door opens. Aimee. I see Anne and Neil behind her; they have brought her to me. Thank you. I ask if Aimee knows. Anne says no.

"Hi, Dad! What are we doing here?" She is puzzled; walks around the cot and kisses me. She knows something's very wrong. Her eyes grow large as she sees Katie in my arms.

"What happened to Katie?"

I can hardly speak; I whisper, "She's okay." I hug Aimee, who puts her thumb in her mouth as she sits next to me.

Here we are. All of us. The DiGiulio family.

But not to Aimee.

"Where's everybody? Where's Mommy? Where's Christine?"

All I can do is swallow. I lay down with Katie in my arms and have Aimee put her head against my other shoulder.

"Aimee, Mommy and Christine…"

I can't speak. She tilts her head, puzzled.

"Aims, Mommy and Christine… they died. They…"

She sat up and stared at me.

"For real, Daddy? Please don't joke."

"For real. Oh, Aimee, I wish it was a joke."

She cried a strange, long, loud wail.

"No, Daddy. Don't joke! Mommy said she wasn't going to die for a long, long time!"

She sucked her thumb again, and laid back on the cot.

She sat up.

"When are we going home? I hate this place!"

"Soon. Just as soon as the nurses say Katie is ready to go."

They confer; tell me Katie could stay another day for observation. I flatly refuse to leave her under any circumstances. Can they roll in a bed for me; for Aimee?

No, they decide. She can be released. Do this for her; do that. Words.

I realize why Valium is so addictive; I feel not calm but slow. I am at the slowest setting on my old record player—16 r.p.m. They walk us out to a car; Paul opens car doors for us and drives away toward home. Like a child, I squeeze my eyes closed as we pass the crash spot on Route 106. Skid marks. Long skid marks.

Yes, Aimee. Grandma and Grandpa died, too. No, I don't believe it either. I hold her hand to prove I am here. She touches Katie's back, probably to prove she is here, too. Nothing can be believed but what we touch.

Food Chrissie started preparing still sits on the stove; fresh wild violets she picked are in a small vase on my piano, next to the music for "The Rainbow Connection," which we were singing the night before, along with "Happy Birthday" to five-year old Aimee.

Somebody mowed the grass. Katie will not let go of me. I will not let go of her. Her perspiration and mine soak my "Super Principal" T-shirt.

Phew. Her hospital diaper needs changing.

I hold my breath as I place her on the table. Paul sits across, waiting for me to look at him. Her diaper comes off; I shrink from her vicious purple abdomen, the crux of a purple welt shaped like a "V" extending to each shoulder. The car seat belts. I tell Paul the doctor thought there was nothing wrong with her internally. The bruises should disappear in about two weeks. Tough kid.

"Look! I learned this in Vancouver," said Paul, grinning. "Bet you can't do it!" I look up and he has dangled a teaspoon by its bowl on the tip of his nose.

It's five o'clock, and the house is gradually becoming jammed with people. Relatives arrive from New York—my brother Tommy. I run out to him. I hug him; his face smells like my Dad's. My sister Ann has brought Mom and her husband, Tom, from Connecticut.

The funeral directors, neighbors, parents of my students, everyone is there. A sea of talking heads like a Bill Gaines crowd scene from *MAD* magazine. The phone is constantly ringing. I'm still at the kitchen table; Katie clings to me like a leech. I see my father-in-law's shoes under the table. Aimee is sleeping on the sofa. The sofa that was a bed for Grandma and Christine this morning. This morning? Impossible. It was years ago.

The funeral director shakes my hand. His huge hand feels like a potholder mitten. Sitting, he opens an envelope and spills out things into his hand. What are they? They look like plastic toy charms in his potholder. He tells me it is Chrissie's wedding band ("Yes. I promise. Till death do us part"), her diamond engagement ring ("Chrissie, is this diamond a 'marquise' or 'marquee'?"), and two cameo earrings, gem-quality European cameos her Dad had had custom-made. The cameo is missing from one earring. He puts everything back in the envelope.

Another envelope. A wallet and car keys.

I am numb; I feel nothing. I can neither cry nor eat. I sit at the kitchen table and hope Paul will keep talking to me. The house is bulging with people. An unfamiliar woman holding my parenting book puts it on the table in front of me. She wants it signed by the author. Paul takes the book and signs on the inside cover, "With best wishes, Robert DiGiulio." I look at the demented man and smile.

ɜ•ɜ•ɜ•

Burial. No viewing hours. No wake, please. Not now. Four blue coffins, each with a small pine-tree design on the lid. People in a box. The priest talks, a baby cries. Katie puts a flower she has picked on one of the coffins.

I hold Aimee by the hand as I carry Katie back to our car to go home.

ɜ•ɜ•ɜ•

Today is Monday. I haven't eaten for three days. Just drank coffee and water. I ate a little yesterday, after they were buried. Everyone is gone. I open a few cards; a few letters. I can't concentrate, and the girls need a bath anyway. I've got to buy something for the tub so the kids don't slip—"appliqués." I'm trying so hard to forget. No, not forget, but I am trying to divert my attention. I cannot read; I cannot write anything more than a check or type an entry in this journal. Typing is automatic. Someone told me the funeral will cost $14,000.

Katie is looking at the full-length mirror on the inside of the bathroom door. She is pointing to the mirror; to her reflection and repeating, "Momma died," as she nods seriously. She is playing with my new metal tennis racket, tapping it on the floor. She and Aimee sleep clinging to me each night. I have to "unstick" myself from them to move or get up. Last night I lay in bed on my stomach and Katie crawled up on my back. She pushed up my shirt and pressed her bare chest against my bare back. It felt odd, but must have been comforting to her, for she immediately fell asleep.

ɜ•ɜ•ɜ•

We visited and stayed with my sister Ann and her husband Frank in Meriden, Connecticut, since late Monday, and drove back today.

At home, I put both girls to sleep in my bed, rolling up blankets like bolster pillows to keep Katie from falling out. As I tiptoed away they looked so peaceful.

Sitting alone downstairs I put my face into the sofa cushions, and, for the first time in my life, I didn't want to live anymore. I was dumb with grief and wanted out. It was ten o'clock. I tried to pray, but fragments of meaningless Catholic-school prayers rolled out automatically. Living just didn't seem important; I tossed around a scheme where I would leave the girls with Ann and Frank and come home alone and...

And what? Kill myself? Kill the guy whose truck rammed them? Kill everyone?

Aimee called out for a glass of water and Katie called for Chrissie. I got water and went upstairs. I picked Katie up as she whimpered, and in anguish we sat in the rocking chair, crying together until morning.

ta ta ta

The necessary business gets us going this morning. I can't find socks for Katie; Aimee has but one pair of clean underpants left in her drawer.

"Mommy said she's going to get me some." Aimee speaks of them in the present tense, talking as if they're still here: "Mommy wants me to... that's Christine's, not yours... Mommy knows I don't like apples..."

"We'll go buy you new underpants, Hon."

We get into the Rabbit, and I buckle Katie into a borrowed infant seat; the old one was destroyed in the crash. As we drive, Aimee asks if our Rabbit can hop; something I did once accidentally by engaging the clutch too quickly. Now it sends her wild with joy to be in the "hoppity Rabbit." This started a familiar game: After I make the Rabbit hop, she then asks where the Rabbit's ears are, and I put the radio on. First one speaker, then another. Then, "honk honk," it talks. Our little game.

When the game ends, it becomes too quiet in the car. I feel heartsick to see Chrissie's empty front seat.

I love them so much. But they are *babies*. They do baby things and ask baby questions and eat and crap like babies. Katie cries, "Out, Dada!" as she strains against the seat-belt straps in the back seat. She hates the car seat just as she did before That Day. No Chrissie to turn around and soothe her. It's so fatiguing being "on call" as a single parent.

I grab for the baby bottle rolling on the floor as I drive and wipe the nipple against my shirt. Here, it's clean. She flings it down.

"Do you want a lolly?" I ask, foolishly before checking to be sure they're here. Check the glove compartment. Were they in my car or in Chrissie's? Nothing. No lolly. Aha—I give her an air-pressure gauge, pulling out the white plastic stem.

"Here, Katie. See? Air gauge for tires and..."

She flings it, bouncing it off my headrest and out the window. In my rearview mirror I see it spinning on the highway like a tiny cheerleader's baton.

The crash site is about a hundred yards ahead. I feel alarm; a knot in my stomach. Thank God I have to turn left now to go to the shopping center. As I make my turn, I see a patch of flattened grass across a small field between the fork in the roads. I am terrified to look at that grass; fearful I will see Christine's doll or Chrissie's missing cameo lying with the shards of glass and strips of steel. I want the grass to grow quickly; I wish someone would go there and rake up the glass and metal.

I'm the only man in J.C. Penney's this morning. How odd to be looking at toddler underwear and teensy socks and the piles of Pampers (Pampers! "Oh, Bob, the picture on the Pampers box doesn't look anything like Christine!") and the lamps with colorful plastic balloons. Strange how I feel warm here, safe among the teddy bears and Playtex nursers. I pick out crew socks for Katie and underpants for Aimee. They will love them. Katie is getting heavy in my arms. Aimee is lost among the Sesame Street–decorated pajamas, sucking her thumb as she strokes a satin hem on her baby blanket. She looks as if she's been crying.

The cashier looks at me and smiles.

"Baby-sitting today, huh, Dad?"

I look at her, nod, and smile. As I hold out the money I want her to touch my hand as she takes the money.

She asks, "These for her?" pointing at Aimee as she holds the underwear. I nod again.

Shakes her head.

"Way too big. They stretch. These'll never fit her. Look at the size..."

She turns over a label and shows me how to find the size.

"Look at this: See? A girl like her would take no more than a five (or was it a six?)." I smile and agree; she walks toward the underwear display, and I follow like a puppy. As I walk I smell the perfume of her hair.

"You men can be so helpless!" she scolds. "What would

your wife say when you brought home the wrong sizes, hmmmmm?"

"Take 'em back," I reply.

I almost told this stranger how alone I felt and how much I wanted to hold her; to have her ride in the car with me.

As we walked to the car, Katie repeated her first phrases: "Momma die. 'Tine die. Momma die. 'Tine die..."

Independence Day, 1980. Compared to New York City, Vermont is tranquil on the Fourth of July. No fireworks, no cherry bombs, no "M-16s." Peaceful. But the loneliness I feel this morning is overwhelming. They are gone one week and one day and I am missing them enormously. I feel physical pain—weak, tired. I can't stop thinking of them for a minute. At home I sit at Chrissie's place at the kitchen table. I can't bear to look at her seat, empty. I've been sleeping on her side of the bed for the same reason. I miss her so much. I am sexually frustrated and at the same time angry at myself for being so... so selfish.

Went to a cookout today; it is still brutally hot. I fix Katie a "hang-in-er" with ketchup as she likes it. I overheard someone say they read in the paper that the truck driver was charged with four counts of vehicular homicide. They said the maximum prison sentence for each conviction could be "life."

I had no trial, yet I am already convicted. I committed no crime, yet I am already serving my sentence. My life sentence.

The radio on the picnic table is blasting. Everything—TV and radio and other people's voices—all seem so loud and intrusive. The WNHV radio announcer is pleased to tell us the National Safety Council has reported no deaths on Vermont or New Hampshire highways so far this Fourth of July weekend.

Katie seems to brood. She shows her grief by her behavior: She clings to me and wants me to sit with her. She seems to fear being by herself. Aimee is different. Simple things can distract her, like the noise of the "peepers," miniature frogs that chirp unendingly at the pond across the road. She asks lots of questions, especially when I put her and Katie to bed. She really doesn't cry much, but when she talks, she has a sad tone to her voice.

"How are you feeling, Hon?"

"Bad. Daddy, was Mommy driving carefully?" she asked.

I looked at her big hazel eyes.

"Yes, she was."

"Why did she have to die?"

"I don't know. But it sometimes happens when..."

"Did the truck driver die, too?"

"No, Aims, he didn't."

"Where is he?"

"I think he's still in the hospital."

"Is he going to die, too?"

"I don't know... he had a... a broken leg, I think... no, I don't think he's going to die."

She thought for a moment; her face darkened.

"Well, I do. I hope he dies, too," she said.

Sunday had been our special day. About a year ago Chrissie and I and the girls began to attend Sunday mass: We were trying to shake off our status as "fallen-away Catholics." But something was still missing—a sense of community, of belonging. Perhaps we had been so alienated by years of Catholic indoctrination that now, in 1980, we had no idea what it meant to be Catholic. Hence, we soon began to drive past the church after giving ourselves permission, ("Do you wanna go?" "Nah. Do you?" "Nah. I'm hungry!"), and we'd continue on to Ludlow where we instituted a new family ritual: having Sunday breakfast together—the five of us—at a bakery/coffee shop called "Sweet Surrender."

We'd sit on low stools looking out through a huge storefront window, turning to see the fantastic baked goods behind us. We'd laugh; we'd talk. It felt so wonderful. We were a cheerful group, and our Sunday breakfast meant so much more to us than attending Sunday Mass.

Did God punish us for skipping Mass? For "falling away" again? I wondered. My seventh-grade teacher, Sister Florence Marie, had told me that God held Catholics to a higher standard because they had had the Truth revealed to them, and thus should know better. To be born and raised ignorant (that is, Jewish, heathen, oriental, et cetera) was no one's fault—at judgment, God would be merciful with those innocent and unenlightened people—they were still His children even though they were uneducated. But culpable were those who had turned their backs on the Truth, once revealed. (This included all Protestants and fallen-away Catholics, whose collective fate after death worried the dickens out of dear Sister.)

Katie is oblivious to the crash That Day. Aimee isn't. She keeps asking me, "Why did Mommy and Christine die? Why did Grandma and Grandpa die? Where are they?"

Aimee also asks me, "Did they *know* they were going to die?" and "Did they *want* to die?"

Hard questions for me to hear. But I am glad they were not too hard for her to ask.

Death is incomprehensible to young children. When Chrissie and I were asked about it, we handled the questions in the same way. I remember the last time when Chrissie was asked by the girls:

"Mommy, are you and Daddy ever going to die?"

"Yes, everyone has to die, but for us it won't be until we're old—for a long, long time."

"How long, Mommy?"

"Oh, pretty long. Years and years and years."

"Who's going to die first? You or Daddy?"

"We're going to both be nice old men and women, just like Grandma and Grandpa," she'd say, reassuring them.

Chrissie would pick them up and wiggle them back and forth as she hugged them.

"Not for a long, long time!"

The day before they died, I was sitting at our picnic table with Christine. I asked her if she would take care of me when I was an old man. She jumped into my lap and told me, "Sure, 'Dada,'" imitating Katie's pronunciation.

"I never want to get married or move away. I'll stay here always with you and Mommy."

Christine didn't like school, either. It was a little embarrassing for me—a school principal—to have a daughter who had to be coaxed and dragged to school. She was bright, and as is true for so many bright kids, she did not tolerate well the restrictions school—even the first grade—placed on her life. As she sat in my lap, she crossed her arms in front of herself and told me, "I *hate* school! I'm not going back!"

"Everybody goes back to school after summer, in September."

"No, I'm *never* going back to school, Dad!"

I hugged her and pressed my nose into that most ticklish crease in her neck.

"We'll see, Toots," I told my little would-be school drop-out.

The last times we were together replay in my mind

constantly, over and again, like that Zapruder film of JFK's assassination replayed countless times. My last day with Chrissie plays over in slow motion, regular speed, and fast motion.

The night before; the birthday party for Aimee at Howard Johnson's in the evening; the afternoon cook-out. My father-in-law's animated face as he gossiped about his co-workers; Chrissie's eyes laughing and her voice yelling as Katie's hot dog was drawn from her little fist by Calico, our neighbor's feisty English springer spaniel.

Don't call this self-pity, because it is true: Widowed people are alone in more ways than people think. It's bad enough that no one is left to share these silly moments, but it's worse when one person must become the archivist—the keeper—of all these memories. And that is another reason why I am writing all this down. It is too hard to remember everything, and for me to unload it onto paper is a relief.

Are they really gone? Are they really... dead? This is a bad joke, a bad dream. Leaving lights on at night helps. In fact, I've been leaving most of the downstairs lights on all night long. The front door is unlocked. They'll be home soon. When they walk in through that door I will look not at them but at Katie and Aimee to see their faces light up. I see Katie clamber off the sofa and run to the kitchen screaming, "Momma! MOMMA! MA-MA-MA-MA-MA'S HOME!!!" I see Chrissie grappling with a loaded brown paper grocery bag as she tries to turn the doorknob, exhaling with relief as she places the bag on the table: "Katie, please! Give us a chance to put this stuff down."

I see Aimee look up from her Dr. Seuss book and dash a few short steps behind Katie screaming, "My Mommy!" in sweet dissonance with her sister. It will be all right when Aimee turns triumphantly to me, takes her wrinkled thumb from her mouth and announces:

"See Daddy? I *was* right. You *were* joking! I *told* you in the hospital Mommy really didn't die! You were just fooling me!"

Christine will have her slightly crooked smile as she drops a brown paper bag on the floor. Like a Slinky, a long loaf of white bread droops and then falls out. "Too heavy for me! Mommy gives me the heavy bags, Dad!" she says, noticing that her Dr. Seuss books have been taken out by her sister without her permission.

"And Aimee, who said you could read my books, hmmmm?"

But Christine just smiles the smile of a long-suffering older sister as Aimee shrugs her shoulders.

And I stand in the living room, looking out the window to the driveway. I see her blue Plymouth there, right behind my white VW. My eyes go from the car outside to my wife, sitting at the kitchen table. Her blouse is unbuttoned with Katie nursing at her breast.

Chrissie will look up at me and smile,

"I'm home, 'Dada!'"

Sleeping is a chore for me. When I lie down I sleep for a couple of minutes to one hour, then wake up with a jolt and roam the house like a zombie.

My dreams are not fun—through my windshield I see a truck ahead of me. Coming fast at me. Or I'm in a hospital and ahead, at the end of a long, white corridor, are swinging doors. I walk as fast as I can but only reach the doors after what seems like an eternity. A doctor stands there and says, no, I may not enter. He tells me Chrissie's condition is very critical, but I could come back tomorrow and try again. After pleading fruitlessly, I walk away. With either dream I wake up with soaked sheets and pillow.

No matter how many times I put them in their own beds, the girls crawl right back into mine.

I put the telephone back on the hook now that the kids are sleeping. And I smoke. Two, three? How many packs a day? Maybe four. Reading is almost as hard as sleeping. Began reading Kurt Vonnegut's new *Jailbird* two days before That Day. It is still opened face-down on my dusty night table. I don't care much about anything, and certainly not about fictitious characters.

෨෨෨

Mary Poppins is at the Claremont Drive-in. We're going tonight.

This morning was lousy. I tried to keep the floor clean by picking up toys constantly; clothing is all over the place. I vacuumed twice, and used the nozzle to push leftover toys out of the way as I vacuumed. The phone rang.

"Good morning, Mr. Dee Goo-leo—I hope I'm pronouncing it correctly. I'm with Fertile Hope Life Insurance and..."

"Sorry, but I don't want any."

"Well, as a married man—you are married, aren't you?— I'm sure you've thought about how your family would survive in the event of your disability or, uh, absence. Now with our low-cost Pioneer..." I hung up and went back to the vacuum.

I stuck the nozzle under the sofa. Thunk. Something stuck in the vacuum.

I looked in the nozzle. Looked like a clump of something. It was the head of a Barbie doll. I banged the nozzle against the floor.

The phone rang again. Paul. I told him I had sucked up a Barbie doll head into the vacuum cleaner. It sounded like he fell off his kitchen stool laughing. I shined a flashlight into the nozzle. Blue eyes twinkling, Barbie smiled at me. It was so ridiculous. Seeing it, and hearing Paul laugh, I laughed so hard tears came to my eyes. It was the first time I had laughed since That Day.

Aimee heard me and came into the room. I showed her the object of my laughter, but she asked,

"Why did you put Barbie's head in there?"

As I drive my car I see a truck coming at me at every curve in the road. I practice jerking the steering wheel—ever so slightly—in case that truck is real. And I "time" telephone poles: At 40 miles per hour it takes four seconds to go to the next telephone pole. That's all they needed: one telephone pole. In either direction. If they had only been four seconds earlier or four seconds later, the truck would have missed them.

One Mississippi Two Mississippi Three Mississippi Four Mississippi

They stopped at the Reading Country Store before going down the road, so why didn't they buy four more seconds of time? The amount of time it takes to read the last sentence aloud! Why didn't they buy a quarter-pound more ham for their picnic? One slice more? Why didn't they buy a quarter pound *less*? Or why didn't my father-in-law pick up *USA Today* or meet a neighbor or have to stop for a tack in his heel? Why did/didn't they buy *one pack of anything*, like Juicy Fruit gum for Christine? Or this: If Chrissie had *not* taken the thirty seconds or so to carefully and responsibly strap Katie into her "Strollie" car seat, they'd all be alive today! The truck would have danced with the trees instead of my wife's car. My fault: Why didn't I fill the tank with gas the day before? If they hadn't had to stop for gas they would have missed the out-of-control truck by ten miles.

why? why? why? why? why? why? why? why?
why? why? why? why? why? why? why?
why? why? why? why? why? why?
why? why? why? why? why?
why? why? why? why?
why? why? why?
why? why?
Why?

We made it to the drive-in; sign says $3.00 per person. A beefy man in the little booth sees the kids in the back.

"And good evening, Dad!" he greets us as he stoops to peer into our car. I jerk my thumb back at Katie.

"You're not going to charge me for the baby, are you?" I only have ten bucks on me.

He smiles and chuckles as he speaks. Why is he so happy, imprisoned in a hot little booth, being eaten by mosquitoes? Why does the caged bird sing? I hold out the ten.

"Nawww! Seeing as Dad got stuck baby-sitting tonight, let's just call it three bucks!" As he turned toward the cash drawer he kept talking to himself. "Jesus, the wife's been on my case to take the kids out but..."

He now seems sad behind his sweaty chuckles.

"...'but hey,' I says to her, 'you're the mother! Hey, I work for a living. Two jobs!'" he adds as he gives me my change.

I wonder: What is his day job? Inseminating cows? Teaching philosophy at Dartmouth?

A car has pulled in behind me as I inch forward.

"Us guys gotta stick together!" I call back as he salutes me with a raised fist.

Mary Poppins was great; I was the only one awake at the end. The drive back was desolate. I felt very lonesome.

Aimee asked me if, when she gets older, she could be Katie's mother. I told her that Aunt Ann, Aunt Paula, and Grandma DiGiulio are a little bit like mothers. In fact, each of them is a real mother. Aimee liked to hear that.

As I write this, the song "How to Handle a Woman" from *Camelot* is playing on the radio. Why do women have to be "handled"?

I have to learn not to be so driven to pick up after the kids. The compulsion to pick up comes from knowing that if I don't pick up or clean up a spill, nobody else will. Sure, Aimee can do little jobs, but she can't do nearly as much as Christine could do, almost two years older. I miss my little Christine so much. So much my chest hurts; my throat hurts. She loved me so much, too. As she sat at my electric typewriter, her fingers would dance on the still keys in fanciful imitation of my typing. Christine wanted to be a writer when she grew up.

True, she didn't want to go to school, but she was looking forward to her Dad being the new principal. She was fiercely protective of her mother, too. Like every oldest child, Christine wanted our approval for all she did. We tried to downplay that; we wanted her to be less dependent upon our constant approval.

I cut the grass again today and trimmed around the white and purple alyssums Chrissie planted. Her violets are getting holes from the bugs (she would lift off bugs one by one and deposit them far away). I think that's part of their life-cycle. Chrissie explained to me how violets are part of a unique family—they bloom twice in summer. Or was it that they have two root systems? Damn. I can't remember what she said.

I got my "perm" today; the perm I had been thinking of getting for months. Looks like a modified Afro. I look in the beauty salon mirror; the young woman behind me under the dryer is totally oblivious to my new look. If she only knew!

I talked on and on, telling the hairdresser how this would have been our tenth wedding anniversary.

She stopped trimming my hair, came around from behind my head, and pointed her comb at me.

"Robert, there are many folks who haven't had one *month* of a happy marriage. Look at it this way: Be happy for what you did have."

School board meeting. I am going to quit as principal; no bombshell, for I told them this a few days ago. Otherwise, the meeting seemed filled with trivia. Lengthy discussion about where to store musical instruments over summer, and whether to hire Lenny, Benny, or Jenny to cut the grass. We sit at student desks arranged in a circle. Impatient, I mindlessly begin to pick at knots and bumps in the wood under the desktop as

I try to listen to the discussion. Gross. I've been stroking wads of fossilized chewing gum stuck under there.

The school board meeting convinced me that very little seems important to me anymore. The girls, and maybe having a date someday with a nice woman. Little else.

I can hear the clock ticking.

I bought a fireproof file cabinet from Sears and it was delivered today. I put all the wedding photos and albums in its bottom drawer, for if the house burned tomorrow, that is one of the few things I would miss.

I just woke up. It's about 5:30 in the morning. I had sat on the floor until 4 a.m. looking at photographs. Feelings went wild. I felt mad—cheated, victimized, and just before I fell asleep on the floor, very sad. Chrissie has been gone nineteen days. This can't be so. It is a joke. A painful joke. Please come back. I need you. I love you.

The girls are napping now on the couch. I set up a small fan, which is blowing torrid air around the living room. Funny how in the winter Vermont can be the Klondike, yet today it's a tropical rain forest.

Yesterday, Katie had an accident on the middle cushion; she should have had a diaper on. I'm trying to get her to use the little plastic potty, which sits in the bathroom next to what Aimee calls "the big-hynie potty." (You never think of a toilet bowl as being huge until you look at it through a child's eyes.) Katie just sits there, getting up every so often and checking her nest like a chicken trying to lay an egg.

I took off the slipcover and shoved it into the washer. Turn the dial. What's the difference between "knit/delicate," "permanent press," and "normal" cycles? Isn't anything you put in the washer normal? How can you have abnormal laundry?

(No bleach. That I know. The colors are mostly red, including the new red towels I bought from Sears. Bleach would annihilate.)

Play safe: knit/delicate.

Uh-oh. The water turned as red as blood. Like in *The Ten Commandments*. I stared hypnotized into the washer for fifteen minutes. It's actually a stunning sight: pink suds riding on red water.

Before Chrissie and I bought the washer, we'd do the laundry at the corner laundromat—The Washing Well on Church Avenue—and it was fun. You bought the little packets of detergent, dumped them in the machine when the little amber light went on, and fabric softener when the other light went on, and take everything out when all the lights went out. Easy!

But the best part was watching "Laundromat Children." In action. Even for Brooklyn they were a dreaded alien species. They entered sniveling, dragged by a loud, frantic Laundromat Mother pulling a shopping cart with, maybe, four pillow cases filled with dirty laundry. Once inside, the Laundromat Children were unremitting—out-and-out holy terrors. We especially liked seeing two Laundromat Children who, tiring of pushing each other around in canvas laundry carts, got into a dryer, closed the round glass door and spun around in the tumbling basket— reminded me of a ride they used to have at Steeplechase in Coney Island. The Laundromat Mother stood outside the dryer bellowing at the children, "That's IT! I'm telling Lenny! If you don't come out, youse don' get no Good Humor tonight. When the man comes around, don' ask me or Lenny for nothin'!"

Today I thought Chrissie was in the room with me. I was rinsing dishes at the kitchen sink and I turned and began to talk with her—"Y'know I'm really surprised that..." I felt a stab of realization, then pain. I realized she was not there. Her presence is so strong that I automatically include her in my daily thoughts and actions. It is hard for me to believe Chrissie is not here.

The day after tomorrow would have been our tenth anniversary. We had planned to go to dinner—by ourselves for a change—and then take a car trip to Maine. Ten years. Tempus fugit. I knew her so completely, yet I hardly knew her at all. She knew me, but in many ways I was a stranger, too. I dream of her almost every night. Again last night I dreamed she was alive but in intensive care. The doctor would not let me go in; they say, "You can see her soon. Not now, but soon."

As I sat with Chrissie at the kitchen table in the days before she died...

(As I write this it looks SO ODD on my typewriter: "before she *died*"... she *what?* Chrissie? My wife? *My wife?* Died? Impossible! She's only thirty-one! Thirty-one-year-old women with three young children and thirty-one-year-old husbands don't just *die!*)

...I told her I was afraid something was going to happen to

us, because we had been unusually fortunate. Several couples and families we knew seemed to be going through difficult times: money troubles, fighting, or problems with children. Chrissie and I were spared those misfortunes. With three healthy children, my first two books published, a new job, and an upcoming tenth-anniversary summer to share, we felt blessed. It troubled me.

Today is hot; it was 87 degrees at ten this morning. Unbelievable. That heat wave has killed over 700 people in the Midwest and South, and it's moving toward New England. Jimmy Carter's buy/rent-a-fan-or-air-conditioner program has been stepped up. You've got to like Carter for being decent. How could someone so non-political have become U.S. President?

The girls enjoyed their new turtle-shaped "Mr. Turtle" kiddy pool, but only after I scooped out a billion dead bugs. Aimee yelled when her foot brushed a bug; outside the pool Katie enjoyed squishing around in the muddy grass, embedding her foot up to the ankle, then lifting it with a 'pwak.' It took a half-hour to clean the pool, fill it with water, and clear it of bugs and mud. There was one bug left. I plucked him out and made believe I put it in my mouth. Aimee screamed and covered her eyes as I chewed. And—gulp—swallowed. "Yummy!" I said.

Finally got it clean, and of course, as soon as I announced it was ready, Katie and Aimee spent all of their time outside the pool, trampling around it, making mud pies and grass pies, and playing 'pwak.' Swell.

They look a little less lost today; more active and cheerful.

Sent the film from Chrissie's camera to be developed.

⋙⋙

I discovered a small diary Chrissie was keeping on a shelf in our room amidst her books. In it was only one entry, a poem she had written:

The magic of my first-born child remains alive within me
Though years have passed and memories dull
I feel the stillness of those nights;
the lullaby of creaking floors,
a bottle warming on the stove—
A dream so real and yet no more

The then and now are fused together,
the middle years seem lost forever,
I look at her and feel the babe tucked in my arms so long,
so very long ago.

There are no days now, only moments—
A lush green scene beyond a window pane
A dream to remember when glistening snows
and dead still nights replace the summer splendor.
I look upon her face, hoping always
to remember every feature of my last, my third—
So amazingly small, so soft—
How bewildered you seem!

Today was not a good day at all. On my way back from Sears in Claremont and as I was making my right turn onto Route 106, I looked to my left across the grassy field. I saw the spot where the crash happened. I wanted to get out of the car, run across the field, and lie on the flattened grass... look through the broken glass, hold it—it was mine, take it home with me.

I want to know. But I don't want to know—ever—what took place at that spot at the last moment of their lives. I want to find Christine's doll, Mom's eyeglasses, and Pop's camera. I want to find the cameo missing from Chrissie's earring. If I don't look now, it will become overgrown and I'll never know.

I got out of the car and slowly walked toward the spot. The heat was shimmering off the pavement. Perfectly quiet. The spot was about a hundred feet ahead on the shoulder by the curve. Only one house was in sight—an old, unpainted farmhouse to the right. A car passed. The sun was hitting me in waves; my head was palpitating. There. What's that? A pull-tab. I stopped and felt dizzy, my head was pounding.

What were they saying? What were they doing as they came to this spot just ahead of me? What did their faces look like as that unseen truck hurtled toward them? They were laughing, I know. Pop was teasing Christine; Mom was telling him, "Oh Paul, leave her alone!"

Christine was imitating, "Yeah, Paul, leave her alone!" Chrissie had both hands on the wheel.

No. I'm feeling dizzy. Can't go look through the grass. Maybe next time.

As Aimee came downstairs this morning, I was vacuuming the living room. The Electrolux sounded funny; it wouldn't pick up any dirt. Oh, yeah. Barbie's head is still in the hose. Only one way to get her out. I shifted the hose's end from vacuum to blower. Perfect. Barbie's head shot out—Pfffffftttt!—and smacked into the wall above the piano.

Aimee, eating Cheerios and watching the proceedings, ran to fetch Barbie's head. She was puzzled and indignant:

"Daddy! Dad! What do you keep doing to my Barbie?"

"Nothing. Remember? Her head was stuck in the..."

"Why did you put her head in the vacuum cleaner?"

We finally found Barbie's headless torso under the sofa and put her back together again.

(How absurd a caricature of womanhood is Barbie. If a human woman had her relative dimensions, she could walk over parking meters without jumping, and would be so top-heavy that she'd topple forward.)

It's official. I quit. I won't be school principal anymore. I have money enough to last till October. Can get a part-time job. No way I'll leave my girls with a sitter while I go off and take care of other peoples' children. Would rather go on welfare and be with the girls than go work at a job and worry about them. I now see why adolescent unmarried girls so frequently bear children without the basic means to support them. When your life is zero empty, children give you something to live for, something to fill the meaninglessness.

They've been gone now for twenty-eight days.

As I burned this week's paper trash, I came across a newspaper that jogged my memory. A few weeks before That Day, Chrissie and I had read about a bus that plunged into the bay in St. Petersburg, Florida. As we rode in the car, she read aloud that a ship had hit the bridge's support columns, breaking the roadway and sending the bus into the water. We talked about how randomly death seemed to strike. It brought to mind the *Bridge of San Luis Rey* where pilgrims plunge to their death when a rope bridge breaks. Why them? Why then? We decided it was an unknowable mystery. A tear came to Chrissie's eye when she read that a young child had died on board that bus. She closed the newspaper and dropped it to the floorboard as she tried to shake the sadness out of her head.

But there is really no way to understand sudden death; it violates our belief that the world is an orderly and predictable place. Children have no such need to see the world as rational.

We adults cannot give up our need to see life as rational, and are much poorer for it.

It's still hard to fall asleep and stay asleep. It is 1:00 a.m. and I am staring at the bedroom ceiling. I go downstairs (here I am again at the typewriter), eat two sandwiches and look through the 1979 *World Almanac*, skimming over the names of the pennant-winning teams in the National League for the past fifty years. I still cannot read anything; find it hard to sustain an interest in reading, and in other people's problems, joys, interests, or lives.

Katie still does that weird thing of climbing on my back as I lie face down in bed, usually watching television. She lifts her shirt and presses her bare chest against my bare back. Katie then turns her head flat on my shoulder blade and sucks her thumb. She seems so contented doing this. Is it some kind of bonding?

રા·રા·રા·

Tonight a friend from college called. Now living "the life every guy dreams of" in Los Angeles, he gave me advice on surviving as a single. In order to make it with women, he said, I had to quickly learn two facts of living the single life. First, he warned, don't ever show a woman you're hungry. Never come on to a "fox" like a wolf. Second, get new clothes, because clothes are important to single people. Married men look like married men because they dress like married men. In parting, he recommended I use *G.Q.* to build a wardrobe.

"What's 'jeek-you'?" I asked.

"Jeez! Don't they have it in Vermont? *G.Q.*, Gentlemens' Quarterly. It's like a modern version of *Playboy*, but without the pictures. It'll show you what duds normal people are wearing. Man, get with it! You can't go fox hunting without the right equipment!"

The girls picked berries today from the bushes behind the house. They both seemed okay, until bedtime. Then Aimee cried for Mom. She cried more than I have ever seen her cry. I just put my arms around her and let her cry. I rocked her. We talked about Mommy; we talked about picking more berries tomorrow.

"Daddy, I miss Mommy so much. I wish she would come back to us."

I told Aimee a funny story I made up about a cat (she loves cats). Because this poor cat could only bark, no other cats would associate with her. They feared her and avoided her. Because she was a cat, dogs chased her. In the middle of winter, and almost frozen, she found a large, old, blind dog in a barn who—hearing her bark and thinking she was a poodle—cuddled up to her and kept her toasty snug. She was so comfortable she began to purr, and purr so loudly other cats came and snuggled up to the kind old dog and cat. It was a silly story and I made it up as I went along. Aimee liked best the barking sounds I made. She sucked her thumb and fell asleep.

Do you ever feel like some adults can be worse than kids? Nobody wants to actually hurt kids, but they can be so stupid. Well-meaning adults can be the worst. They have a wide range of ready answers as to why the girls' mom, sister, and grandparents died: "because God wanted them," "because it was 'their time'," "because they were good, and God wants all good people in heaven with him."

Do you ever feel like spiting the world? I do. Given what has happened, I want to see Aimee and Katie grow up to be healthy. To be successful and happy adults. And to have a successful, happy childhood, in *spite* of what has happened. I swear they won't be cheated out of that.

Today I got a sympathy card from the publisher of my paperback book. Inside it read:

> The souls of the just
> are in the Hands of God.
> In the sight of the unwise,
> they appeared to perish,
> but they are in Peace.

Receiving that spiritual card yesterday must've been meant to prepare me for today. We all went to Burger King for lunch. Aimee asked again "if Mommy could see us." She wonders if Chrissie is hiding somewhere. Aimee kept looking up at the skylights, pointed to them, and asked if Mommy could see us through those windows.

I said no, I didn't think so.

She then asked me, "If God loves Mommy, why did he want her to die? If you love somebody you don't want bad things to happen to them."

Someone (remember what I said about stupid, well-meaning adults?) at the Bible School had told Aimee her Mommy was a very good woman, and God wants all good people to be with him.

"No, Aimee, God did not 'want' your mom to die. All people are good." (I resolve now to pull her out of that program tomorrow morning.) "Some good people die young, and some good people die when they are old."

Aimee looked at the huge, potted ferns hanging above us under skylights. She pointed at them.

"Dad, are those plants living?"

I told her yes.

"Are they going to live always?" she asked.

"No, the ferns die, too. All living things die eventually."

"But plants don't die 'by accident,' do they?" Before I could answer, she asked, "Does God want plants to die? Did God want Mommy with him?" she persisted.

"No, I don't think so. I think Mommy is at peace, and I don't think God 'wants' us to die. Everything must die at some time. It's just that dying is part of living, and..."

"Can I get a Happy Meal?"

"This isn't McDonald's. Want a Burger King Kid's Meal?"

"What kind of surprise is inside?"

Going shopping with young children is no problem, and taking them to the restroom is also easy... if you're a mother. Or if you're a father with sons. But what about a father with daughters? Today I realized this little-known fact: It's okay for mother to bring little Johnnie into a woman's restroom, but it's taboo for fathers to bring a daughter into a men's restroom. So there's no place for them to "go"; worse, there's no place for me to "go," short of leaving them outside alone to wander the store.

I didn't know about them, but I couldn't wait.

I stood Aimee outside the men's room door.

"Aimee, you wait right here and hold Katie's hand. I'll be right out!" I flew in and out. Aimee said now *she* had to use the restroom. The woman behind the counter at Burger King overheard and offered to take Katie and Aimee into the women's room. Problem solved, but the question remains...

On to Kmart and its blue-light specials. (I intentionally took the girls to Burger King first because they really like eating at the Kmart cafeteria, which I absolutely detest.) I sat Katie up on the customer service counter as I was getting a check approved. She had a severely chocolate face from a movie-theatre-sized KitKat candy bar.

"Katie," I said in that asinine public voice of parents who lurk at Kmarts and laundromats, "I just don't know how you get so dirty! I just dressed you a little while ago."

The cashier laughed as she ran her finger down the loose-leaf-bound list of check-bouncers who fashioned their own blue-light specials. She pointed at Katie's brown, smeary face and dirty shirt.

"Mommie's gonna make Daddy do the laundry today!" she teased.

Fortunately, Aimee was just out of earshot, because she would have told the cashier The Truth.

Tonight as I rocked Aimee in the huge rocker, she asked about berries again. She seems to want to do the things she did with her sisters before this happened.

"Sure!" I said. To her. To myself it was "Oh, no, not again! Boring! Picking berries is boring!"

She looked up at me, brushed her damp hair from her eyes, and her expression lit up.

"Can we take baskets? Can we take two—no, three baskets? One for you, one for Katie—a little one—and one for me?"

She had an eager sound in her voice.

"But it's raining, Aimee," I said, hoping the glee in my voice was hidden.

"Well, then we can pick berries in the living room, Dad!"

The living room?

"Yeah, here Dad," as she took two baskets and gave me one. Heading into the living room she swept her hand before the sofa and wood stove.

"Look at all those berry bushes!"

For the next ten minutes, Aimee and I—soon to be joined by Katie—"picked berries." Watch the thorns! Yum, don't keep eating them, Katie. Oops! Dropped some.

Make believe actually felt good.

Andy Warhol once said, "In the future everyone will be famous for fifteen minutes." Here comes my chance: I'll be on television—Channel 5 from Boston—this Wednesday. And I should read my book so I know what I'm talking about.

Since That Day, Katie has been subdued. She clings to me; she frequently wants me to hold her (which I do), and she doesn't enjoy being out of my sight for long periods. She still comes into my bed, crawls onto my back and falls asleep there almost every night. I think she is in grief, yet unsure of what has happened here. The physical closeness must be very comforting and reassuring to her.

Aimee and Katie and I wound up having a marvelous day today. We went to Hanover, and spent most of the time walking around the green near Dartmouth College. The best part was the Dartmouth Book Store, which is to books what Disney World is to amusements. Yet the day did not begin well. I told the girls they could each choose a book. Aimee was irascible.

"Book?" she yelled as if I had told her to eat tofu, "I want a TOY!"

(A toy? This is Dartmouth, not Brooklyn. We are surrounded by people wearing expensive prep-school educations. Their children have pursuits, not toys.)

Naturally, she had to add, loudly, "I hate books, Dad." (Dad? Who, me?)

"But," I gasped, "you read so well."

"I want something to play with. I hate to read!"

I walked them both outside, then promptly back into the bookstore when I realized Katie was holding three, unpaid-for copies of *Babar*. Back outside we stopped for a nutritious lunch of greasy egg rolls and salty hot dogs from Hanover's pushcarts.

Food. What a perfect answer! Yes, they were hungry.

"Dad, I'm sorry I acted bratty in the store."

"That's okay, Aims. I get grouchy, too, when I'm hungry."

Katie was sucking her thumb and holding my earlobe with her other hand. My earlobe felt slimy. I touched it. It smelled like an egg roll.

"But, Dad," Aimee continued, "I really do want to get those crayons—the ones you can use in the bathtub."

Okay, crayons for the bathtub. We went back to the Dartmouth Book Store and got the soap crayons ("to share! One set or nothing at all!"). They actually looked like fun. I resolved to try them out when the girls were sleeping.

Unfortunately, all the way home (twenty-plus miles) Katie—who was tired from all the walking—screamed, "I want my Momma! I want my Momma!" as she squirmed to get out of the car seat.

Aimee talked to her. To no avail.

"Dad, could you stop the car? Katie's giving me a 'heddick'."

I stopped the car and walked her around a bit which helped her, as I was cursing under my breath. But when I strapped her back in, she picked up right where she left off, ceasing only as we pulled into the driveway.

We went directly to the bathroom to try out the crayons. The box showed a smiling boy and a girl in a tub drawing like Michelangelos of the Toilet. I filled the tub with water and a smiling Aimee and sleepy Katie jumped in. The crayons were a gyp, making streaky colored smears on the tile and turning the bath water rusty brown.

I feel especially vulnerable to the telephone. Without Chrissie, I must answer the phone each time it rings. Aimee does once in a while, but she's not yet able to handle a conversation. So it takes up a lot of my time—a lot—talking on the phone. The most annoying calls (aside from the calls from people trying to sell me something) are the How-is-Bob-doing? calls.

I'm fine. Fine. Fine. Fine. Fine. Fine. Fine. Fine. Fine. I'm just fine I'm just fine I'm just fine I'm just fine doing well doing well yes getting sleep yes getting sleep no thanks I'm fine no thanks I'm fine no thanks I'm fine take care bye.

I'm vulnerable to scheduling everybody's life. I never kept the calendar for the family: who's doing what, who's going where, whose dental appointment is when, et cetera... When people drop by or come to visit, the social burden is one hundred percent on me now. ("Come look at my new rug! Isn't it nice? So how is Fred doing with his gout? Can you believe how much our taxes will be going up?" and so on.) I see what single mothers have to contend with each night: They come home from work and face a barrage of phone calls, schedules, and responsibilities; especially tough when all the roles fall on one parent. When the girls' friends come over, it's me who's got to say:

"Stay outside! I'm washing the floor!" (Response: "Do we hafta?")

"Stay inside! It's raining!" (Response: same as previous)

"Sarah, please share that toy with Katie!" (Response: "But I haddit first.")

"Time for lunch!" (Response: "Not hungry!")

"Delicious peanut butter and jelly!" (Response: "Jelly? Oh. My mother puts honey on peanut butter sandwiches. Jelly has bad sugar in it, but honey is...")

"Judith, use your fingers on the piano, not cars!" (Response: "They're not 'cars,' they're trucks.")

And it's me who's got to hear:

"Dad, is there anything on TV?"

"Dad, can you send Kevin home? He's swearing!"

"Mr. D, did your wife crash into the truck, or did it crash into her? Stephanie said her mother told her..."

"Mr. D, my Mommy said I can't eat this hot dog because we're veterinarians now."

"Dad, by mistake Michelle 'went' on the bathroom floor."

And getting rid of people is hard to do, too. I don't have Chrissie's knack for getting rid of people gracefully. I put aside what I must do just to talk with someone. Like a million other faceless homemakers, I enjoy and crave the company of adults, yet there is a mountain of things needing to be done.

When that time comes, putting the phone off the hook works well. I do it from 8:30 to about 10:00 every evening so I can get the girls bathed and ready for bed without being interrupted. Fortunately, phones left off the hook here in Vermont do not squawk like demented parrots as phones in New York City do.

Last night was a landmark of sorts. The first night Katie and Aimee went back into their own bedroom to sleep. I put the Sears side rails on Christine's old bed, and Katie now sleeps there. This way I can put the crib away (for the third time) and don't have to be pained by the sight of Christine's empty bed. The two beds go together nicely, one on either side of the doorway.

They still cried a little before bedtime, but as usual, I sat with them and read them (very boring) stories till they fell asleep. "DiGiulio's Law": A bedtime story's ability to interest a child is directly proportional to the speed with which the adult reader is bored to tears by it. Tomorrow night I should read to them from the *1980 National Football League Yearbook*. How do I feel? Cheated. When I read to them I feel warm but cheated.

Dirty kitchen floor. Took out the mop and turned on the Grundig shortwave radio. Radio Moscow!

"...and now the news:" A thin voice of a woman speaking perfect English. Did I realize, she asked, that Odessa and Baltimore are sister cities? She told me the state of Maryland desires a decrease in East-West tensions and that a proclamation had been issued, certifying a bond of friendship between Maryland and the USSR. In Canada, Vancouver was Odessa's sister city: "The peoples of Vancouver and Odessa share in the glorious celebration of friendship as siblings," she said.

Although this was supposed to be the world news, there was no news. Instead, the lead story trumpeted the "glorious celebration" of thirty-five years of friendship between Poland and the Soviet Union. But the best comments were the closing tirades against "theWest," "forces of imperialism," and the "free enterprise system." She never mentioned the United States by name. The "on-the-scene" reports sounded so rehearsed, read directly off a script. Our U.S. news is not news but entertainment; the Soviet Union's news is not news but bullshit.

The funniest Soviet news item was a sports update on the 1980 Olympics (which the United States is boycotting). The announcer raved about "evidence of notable superiority of socialist countries" in yesterday's Olympic boating event held in Tallinn, Estonia. He said the top five finishers were East Germany, Poland, Bulgaria, Romania, and the USSR—all communist countries. But when I read about the event in today's *New York Times*, I learned that those five nations were the *only entrants* in that boating event! In the hour it took me to wash and wax the floor I counted six "glorious-es," three or four "imperialisms," and a few "intractables." Life sounds so grim in Iron Curtain countries. It is difficult to understand why they don't rise up and say, ENOUGH!

❧❧❧

It's been a month. Impossible. I just can't believe a whole month has passed. What did I do from then until now? Where did I go? What the hell happened to July of 1980?

This is early Sunday morning as I write. Beautiful sunrise brightening the sky. But there will be no trip to our favorite bakery, Sweet Surrender, with Chrissie and Katie, Aimee and Christine for sticky buns and coffee.

Katie and Aimee are now playing on the floor behind me as I type. I feel comforted when they are near me, within my sight and hearing.

They're making believe they're at the movies, using their plastic "little people" perched on the keys of my old manual typewriter on the floor.

From the kitchen radio I hear Anne Murray singing "You Needed Me."

Thank God for Bufferin. It helps my daily headache a little.

As Katie and Aimee play in the living room, once in a while Katie calls Aimee, "Mommy." Aimee is protective of Katie. She tells her little sister to take a crayon out of her mouth. Aimee doesn't let Katie go near the driveway. But I don't want Aimee to become a replacement mother.

Here's Katie, now stroking my arm while she sucks her thumb. This morning she tried to play with my nipple, just as she did while nursing with Chrissie. Sometimes while nursing, Katie would playfully pull at a mole on Chrissie's breast, smiling sadistically when her mother yelled in pain.

I just received the photographs in the mail from the roll of film that was in Chrissie's camera. I first put the snapshots away, unopened, unseen. Then I opened the drawer. And looked. Pictures of Katie. A kewpie-doll pose with Katie's hands behind her head and knee bent slightly. Poop-oop-e-doop! Pictures of my mother-in-law, Olga, and my father-in-law, Paul. Only one picture of Chrissie: her serving birthday cake at Katie's birthday party.

It's 11:25 p.m. as I write this, and I've just finished typing my new will from a book on how to write your own will. This is so the girls have a guardian who will love them and treat them well. I've named my sister Ann and Chrissie's sister Paula as guardians. It is comforting to know that if I die, the girls will be loved. Although a will is no guarantee things will be carried out as you wish, without one, courts and lawyers will step in and anything can happen.

When I was a school principal and called to court in guardianship and custody battles, I saw how tense things get after the legal system gets involved. As an educator, you always work toward helping quarreling children reconcile their differences by talking with each other, by listening to the other person's feelings, by being truthful, and by empathizing—seeing the other person's viewpoint. However, our legal system has no time for this; it simply directs people to take sides *against* each other. Sides that quickly become hardened and adversarial. What's the first thing a lawyer tells you to do after he steps in? He tells you *not to talk to* the other guy. In our English/American legal system, to be conciliatory is to be foolish. To give, or to admit to even the slightest fault, places your case in peril. So to the eventual loser (and there must always be a loser when adversarial sides are taken), this guarantees that any verdict will be—and remain—painful, and be seen as unjust.

I have always wondered how different our legal system might have been had it been founded by women instead of by Englishmen. Men construct and use weapons in war, and they construct and use words as weapons in their courts. The goals are the same as in war: to produce victory, to win; to defeat an opponent... somebody... anybody, even if it's your wife or your child.

Speaking of women, Grandma DiGiulio and Aunt Ann came to baby-sit as I went to Boston with Paul. Tomorrow I'll be on the "Good Day" show. My nervousness feels good, so much better than feeling numb and nothing.

We're here in Boston. I'm writing this at the Marriott, and I can't sleep (what else is new?). On television is the movie "10." Bo Derek looks like a mannequin, a Barbie doll. We Americans have a strange idea of female beauty. How can women with severe, plastic faces be considered beautiful?

We live in a sexually segregated society—a world of men and a different world of women. Only occasionally do we take peeks at the other world. And when we do, all we see are superficial images. If men are "trained" on pictures of women, they will never get to know women. For if all a man knows are images, when he meets a real woman he meets only a face, a body; an image.

Furthermore, is beauty—even true beauty (unlike Bo Derek)— a required basis for a man to be happy with a woman?

The saddest part is that so many women, it seems, pursue the same mannequin mentality in seeking their "ideal" man, their "Mr. Right," based on looks. Instead of helping men see that Playboy centerfolds are no more accurate representations of a woman than a picture of Snow White or a statue of Venus, a generation of women is hearing that "it's only fair" that women ogle men as men ogle women, because men ogle women.

Worst of all, this makes it so difficult to come to know someone. Makes us think in terms of height, weight, color, buttocks, biceps, chins, tits, and toes. Thus we evaluate each other's appearance instead of know (and accept the reality of) each other's person.

It's now 11:30 p.m. I can't sleep, I crave caffeine, and I'm famished. The Marriott's coffee shop is closed, so I'm going to prowl around. It is raining furiously.

Howard Johnson's. They have a HoJo right across the street. As I write this at the counter, a very fat man sits two seats away and has just been given a foot-tall malted, a platter with three hamburgers, and a separate, huge bowl of fries. This is true: On Sunday, Mama DiGiulio used to put out the meatballs for our family of five in a bowl the size of the one containing his fries.

I'll order a hamburger. One. I'm so dainty.

The waitress is smiling; she plants both elbows on the counter and looks at me with gentle, soft brown eyes.

"So you're another one afraid of thunder," she joked.

"Yeah. It's pouring out there."

"Nights like this I don't mind being stuck behind this counter. What'll you have, sweetheart?"

Sweetheart... Dear God, I wanted to slowly lean forward and kiss her gently. Her cheek was soft; her lips dark.

Wait. She took a deep breath.

She wanted me.

She leaned closer.

She held her head in her hands and her eyes smiled.

I had to talk to her. To tell her.

I don't know you but I could love you. May I start by gently kissing you? You see, I'm very lonely, and I dearly would love to hold you tonight. I am... well, my wife, see, my wife died last month. No, no, don't move away! Yes, I *know* you're sorry—so am I. Push it aside—that's not important now. No, I'm not looking for a replacement! Are you nuts? It's you. Look. Look at you. Your face is a gemstone; so smiley, soft and kind. And your eyes! What tenderness and strength they have! It's *you*, can't you see? The little I know about *you* I absolutely love. Lean closer, please. Let me smell the perfume in your hair; your neck, your shoulders.

"Do you want the platter with the burger? It comes with fries and coleslaw, or you can have it plain."

I breathed out. And nodded.

"Yes."

"Yes you want the platter, or yes you want it plain? You

want to think about it and I'll come back?"

Then go away! You and I had a chance at something so special. But do you care? No, you and that stupid hamburger platter. Wait. Don't go away. Come back. Look. You don't have a wedding band on; you and I are *the same*—we're available! Can we give it a try? I won't pay attention to your raspy-sounding voice—a minor flaw I can disregard immediately—if you promise to stay here and let me kiss you. I dearly would love to hold you tonight. My sweetheart, call me "sweetheart" again. Lean closer, please. Let me touch your neck, your lips...

"The platter, please. And coffee."

Tomorrow, I'll be famous. Yes, I want you to share it all with me! To hell with HoJo and hamburgers! You would? Then tell me your name! Mine's Bob. I don't think I have the courage now to get married again. At least, not now. Does that matter to you? You have children? So do I! Great—they'll all get along great. But it's time now for us. Take off the apron and hold my hand. Let's get so far away from this. I want to spend time just looking at you and kissing you, uh... what was your name?

"Uh, sir, would you like anything else?"
Yes.
"No, just the platter and coffee, thanks."
I swallowed my coffee. She left to wait on an old lady whose head was shaped like a huge *Rice Krispie*.
I left my sweetheart a three-dollar tip.

After breakfast, Paul and I checked out of the Marriott and went to the Channel Five studios. Got there at 7:45 a.m.
Big Mistake: If you're going to be on TV, don't get there too early. Worst error possible. Had over two hours with nothing to do but get nervous. I paced, smoked, drank tanks of coffee, and the worst part was that I reviewed over and over in my mind what I wanted to say.
Right before I went on, I saw Jason Robards come into the studio.
My moment in the sun was over almost instantly. Paul

timed it: I was on for eight minutes! Eight minutes? Hey, Andy Warhol, they owe me seven more minutes!

When I came off, Jason Robards went on. A moment later, he was yakking away on the air promoting his new film *Raise the Titanic!* which opened today in Boston. Sounded like a dreadfully boring flick. And what a bizarre scene on the set: Robards sitting there with the host and a tiny, shriveled old man—supposedly the oldest survivor of the Titanic disaster. He looked ill at ease, wet and squid-like beneath the television lights. (Where did they get him? Out of the sea? The lengths they go to in promoting a flick.) Off the set, Robards stood across the hall from me. He chain-smoked and hoarsely complained to his agent, "I didn't have enough time! There were a lot of points I wanted to make. I just didn't have enough time!" He sounded pissed.

We never have enough time, Jason.

Come to think of it, it was damned appropriate to put me on immediately prior to a piece on the Titanic.

After the show, I was interviewed over a fancy lunch by a journalist from the *Boston Globe*... ah, fame!

But all I could think of was my waitress. Had she been waiting for me to make the first move? What's the key? How do single people show someone they like them? Being married for ten years has been a handicap.

When we got back to Vermont, my sister and mother told me how Aimee broke into a broad grin when I mentioned her name on the air. Upon seeing my image on the screen Katie jumped up and down, screaming "Dada! That my Dada!!"

"How did I look on TV, Aimee? Did my beard look too long?"

"No, Dad, you looked great! But I like you better like this," she said, hugging my leg.

PART TWO: THE MIDDLE TIME

Death ends a life but it does not end a
relationship, which struggles on in the
survivor's mind toward some final resolution,
some clear meaning, which it perhaps never finds.
—Robert Anderson

One month. I'm now in August without my Chrissie and
Christine. It should not be this way. It feels wrong to start
something new without them, even something commonplace
like a new month.

Where am I now?

On the edge of a precipice. A cliff. Behind me is shock and
numbness; ahead is pain and loneliness. I am past Stage One. I
know the fog is lifting, and I'm afraid of the pain that lies
ahead. As I look back, last month was "Novocain Month." I
was numb, on automatic pilot. Now I feel depressed almost
constantly. Everything is distressing: Daily telephone calls.
Seeing junk mail addressed to "Mrs. Chris DiGiulio." Asinine
television shows. Stupid people at stores and drivers on roads.
Even kind people offering sympathy are unbearable. All of it is
tormenting, including telephone calls from well-meaning
people, asking me how I'm getting along.

"Fine, fine. Things are going well," I lie. I lie because I want
to save *them* from feeling bad for me. People admire me:

"Bob, I don't know *how* you do it!"

"Bob, I don't know *what* I'd do if Joan (Ben/Marie/etc.) were
to die!"

"Bob, I don't know *where* you get your strength!"

"Bob, I don't know *who* else could bear up so well. God
only gives us what we can bear."

"Bob, I don't know *why* this happened."

Shut the hell up.

Most irritating are those who tell me,
"It's okay to cry, Bob. Men are allowed to cry, too."
I know. *I know*. I don't need your permission to cry.

Grief is a no-win situation. If I tell them, yes, I'm in pain,
they feel sorry for me. But if I lie and tell them everything is
fine, they tell me how happy they are I'm feeling well. And
then I feel worse because it's all fake.

Someone who read my *When You Are a Single Parent* book
wrote me a letter. She heard about the crash and told me "the
first year is the hardest; it takes three years before numbness
and anger finally go away." She had been a widow for ten
years, and she said her life had changed, taken on new
meanings: "You don't ever forget," she wrote, "but you do get
better."

Today has not been a good day. I feel isolated. The
distractions of Jason Robards, the "Good Day" show, doing
Boston with Paul, and my HoJo waitress all seem so far away. My
new TV suit is in the closet. It's a letdown after being on TV.

The floor is waxed. I woke up at dawn to do it. It took my
mind off my despair, but I hate that I miss Chrissie when I
struggle with housework, when taking care of the girls, and in
trying to do things she did. I miss her so much. I feel desperate
at times, closing my eyes and feeling her hand on my arm. I
feel it right now.

What scares me is that I must actively come up with
meanings for my life now. I used to just live life. Without
thought, like breathing or walking. Now, life is hard. I question
why I am washing the floor. I ask myself why I appeared on
television. Who cares? WHO GIVES A DAMN? The only thing
I am glad for is people. As bad as my life feels now, people
have been caring. Since the crash many people have told me
"If you need anything, Bob, just call." And if I do call and ask
them to watch Katie so I can go to the dentist, or if I ask them
to drive Aimee to school, or help me hoist a ladder to the roof,
they'll jump at the chance. People have been wonderful—
supportive and nurturing.

But I miss the meaning of marriage. The closeness. Did
somebody ever do something for you without your asking;
something that was exactly what you needed?

If only men and women could just sit still for a moment

and get to know each other. It means temporarily putting aside personal needs and it means listening. To feelings, not words.

Unfortunately, getting our own needs met has become such a national obsession that we have little time to listen to the feelings of another.

Last night I told Paul about my fantasy: a trip to Europe or Hawaii or anywhere, and—most important—finding an amicable woman to share it with me. How exciting is anticipation!

I thought of taking my fantasy a step further by maybe placing a personal ad in the newspaper. How might I describe myself?

"Widowed father, 31, with two children, am now unemployed but will get back to work soon..." No.

"Widowed author (ah! *that* sounds impressive!), 31, loves music, rain, children..." Corny.

"Widowed man, 31, with two amazing daughters, ages two and five. Let me tell you about them..." De-emphasize kids.

"Professional man, 31, educator..." Nah, sounds too dry.

"You, 25–40-year-old woman who loves love, children, music. Me, 31-year-old man who..." Sounds dopey.

"Man, 31, named 'Bob' wishes to meet woman, 31, preferably one named 'Chris' or 'Chrissie'."

I never realized how incredibly difficult it is to describe myself, and describe qualities I seek: kindness, warmth, caring, sensitivity... What woman believes she does not possess any of these? What man believes he does not possess these?

Balanced the checkbook tonight after more than two months' accumulated bank statements and canceled checks. I fear seeing checks Chrissie wrote. Tonight I turned over the last check she wrote; it was to pay for the gasoline that was in her car that day.

I looked closely at the check. Her soft, light handwriting. The way she wrote her name; the little swirl at the top of the *C* and feathery strokes at the ends of words. She used to sit across from me at the kitchen table as I balanced the checkbook. We'd have coffee... I'd look up and comment... how the Favorite Fashions store must dash to cash our check... how Grand Union seemed to wait weeks before depositing our check... how one of our baby-sitters seemed to hold onto her checks for months and months and then fold them into a half-inch square before cashing them... Tonight I feel melancholy, really missing her.

When I went to put the checkbook back in the cabinet, Chrissie's Red Cross cards and cardiopulmonary resuscitation certificates all fell out onto the floor. CPR. A month before she died, she had completed a rigorous course in CPR and life-saving, and now her badges and certificate had just fallen out of the cabinet onto the floor.

This whole thing seems stupid. Okay, you win. I give up. GOD, PLEASE CALL OFF THE JOKE.

Her unfinished work: laundry-room cabinets she was painting gloss white; miniature furniture she was gluing together; her violet and alyssum garden; her "rock garden" that was a garden full of rocks.

And her unfinished children.

And me, her unfinished husband.

Goddammit, you had *no right* to leave us.

None.

There are *your* things. I feel like yelling your name.

The girls are sleeping (on the sofa again despite my new plan for bedtime), and I don't want to wake them. But the scream is there. I want to scream her name like I've never done before, but I am afraid... no, I want to *save* that scream. Because when I'm truly desperate, I want to have ammunition. It's all I will have. It hasn't beaten me yet.

How can she not be here? She was *just here*, wasn't she?

Where did she go?

Why did she go?

How come I didn't know about it?

Why didn't she tell me?

Why did she take our Christine? *Why did she?*

Another hour spent on stupid laundry again. Crap. An hour just sorting through a mountain of clothing—can't tell the difference between Aimee's clothes and Katie's. Is this the way it is for mothers? Can a woman tell a five-year-old kid's sock from a two-year-old kid's sock? How about underpants, and undershirts? They all look the same: Very small. And inside out. Do children do that on purpose? Just to test parental love? Should I leave them that way and have them put them on inside out so that when they are dirty and the girls take them off inside out they will really be right side out?

While I'm on the subject, is it normal for a two-year-old girl to take off her socks and shoes just as you're ready to go out the door with her? Even after you've spent a half-hour getting her dressed? Katie seems to reach that point at the precise moment I say, "Okay. Let's get into the car; we're going to the supermarket." Poof! Off come the socks and shoes. They fly off.

And the grin. I would think it was only my imagination but for her wicked smirk!

Good news today. I was asked to speak to a PTA group next month. The PTA president heard "a local author" was in their midst; would I come talk to them about parenting, and how I got started in writing?

How did I get started in writing?

Paul Robbins got me started. I can even pinpoint the day three years ago. A freelance writer, Paul had been asked to write a piece on summer sports camps. He invited me to accompany him to the Joe Namath Football Camp in Dudley, Massachusetts. I agreed, but as a kid raised on the streets of Brooklyn, I knew I wouldn't relate to it at all. It was one of those rich kids' summer sport camps named for a Really Famous athlete who never set foot near it, except to collect his percentage.

Not quite. There was Namath addressing hundreds of silent, adoring campers seated in a huge field house. When he finished, we broke for coffee and refreshments as hundreds of boys converged upon him.

Later, as Paul and I were walking on a path to the parking lot, we saw him. Coming toward us.

Joe Namath. Alone. Carrying a cup of coffee.

Paul nudged me, "Go ahead, talk to him."

I was incredulous. "No way! Are you nuts? What would I say to him?"

Paul said, "Say, Hi, Joe!"

As Namath approached he smiled. At us.

I nervously said, "Hi, Joe!"

He stopped and said, "Hey, how are you?" Spoken as if he had known me for years.

And I repeated, "Yeah... Hi, Joe! Hello. I'm fine, great!"

I soon found my tongue. "Good luck with the L.A. Rams!"

"Why thanks," he said. He spoke really slowly. "I'm looking forward to it."

We exchanged more small talk as Paul snapped pictures, then Broadway Joe went his way.

(Until that day in 1977, the only Really Famous person who had ever spoken to me was Jerry Lewis at Yankee Stadium in 1963. When I asked for his autograph, Jerry Lewis forged straight ahead, and in his famous nasal voice he chimed, "Sarry!")

A few days later, Paul came by to give me a framed 8 x 10 glossy of Joe Namath and me, both of us holding cups of coffee and talking like close friends.

But I had no idea that a week later that picture would also appear on the front page of our local newspaper, the *Vermont Standard*.

Paul had sent it in, and even provided the caption beneath:

"New Jobs—Robert DiGiulio (left), newly named principal of Bridgewater School, and National Football League great Joe Namath chat for a few moments at Namath's football instructional camp at Nichols College in Dudley, Mass. Like DiGiulio, Namath has a new job... unlike Namath, DiGiulio will not be receiving $175,000 in his new post..."

I called the newspaper to get extra copies. An editor (who liked the picture and concluded that I was a writer like Paul) asked me to interview a local personality for his newspaper. My first by-line.

Later that year I wrote my first magazine article: A piece on managing children's classroom behavior, written for *Teacher* magazine. I Scotch-taped the $250 payment check to the wall by my desk. That is, until I needed money and carefully unstuck it. I made a photocopy of the check and framed it.

On weekends after Chrissie and the girls had gone to sleep, I fleshed out ideas from my notes written on my observations of child behavior, and organized them into a book for parents, which I called *Effective Parenting*.

When it was almost completed in late 1978, I sent a letter around to book publishers, offering to show them sample chapters. I soon had a file folder filled with more rejection slips than Joe Namath had popcorn poppers. Or panty hose.

However, one afternoon I got a call:

"Mr. DiGiulio? This is Abbey Press in Indiana. We looked at your manuscript and I'm sorry to say we decided it's just not for us. But we would like to know if you would write a book on single parenting for us. Are you interested?"

My spine tingled.

"Absolutely. Would love to!"

"Fine. Just let me ask you a few questions."

Naturally, his last question was:

"You are a single parent yourself, aren't you?"

My heart sank. I wasn't. They'd *never* let me do it—no credibility!

He put me on hold to go to another call. I looked desperately at Chrissie. "Damn! He wants to know if I'm a single parent!"

She thought, then brightened, "Tell him we'll get a divorce if they publish your book!"

I did, he laughed, and I wound up writing *When You Are a Single Parent* in the space of four weeks in July.

Within a few months and a couple of revisions, my single parenting paperback became a reality in 1979.

That was good, but my *big* one—my original *Effective Parenting* manuscript—was still waiting for a bite.

This is also a true story: Toward the end of 1979, I came home exhausted from a long day at school. Around four-thirty, I collapsed on the sofa.

The phone rang.

Christine and Aimee raced for the wall phone. Neither could reach it, so—as was their habit—they grabbed a kitchen chair and pushed it toward the phone. One grabbed the telephone receiver, but in her enthusiasm, the other daughter pulled it from her hands. Naturally, daughter #1 was upset, and, as #2 spoke into the phone, #1 was berating her.

"You had no right to pull that out of my hands..."

Bicker, bicker.

"...and I'm going to tell Dad."

On cue, I got off the couch and roared, "That's it! I've had it! I'm trying to nap and you can't even be quiet? Both of you—sit on the couch NOW!"

The phone banged against the chairs, which I fell over as I tried to grab the receiver swinging against the wall.

"WHO IS THIS?" I demanded, seeking to avenge myself on this person who not only started all this ruckus, but who was also a listening Peeping Tom, eavesdropping into the TRUTH of my family life!

A friendly voice asked, "Mr. DiGiulio? Sounds like you have an active family."

"I suppose so. Who is this?" I repeated.

She gave me her name. "I'm managing editor at Follett Publishing Company in Chicago. We *loved* reading your manuscript *Effective Parenting*, and we're interested in publishing it."

Since the time my books were published, parents have told me how powerless they feel. Someone said that raising a child is like watching a movie: the parent is in the audience, squirming and yelling at the screen as the child acts out his part, not hearing the cries from his audience.

I think we Americans are so hung up on controlling our kids. What other country has as many books written to help parents "mold" their children? If only we could simply *be with* our children, and try neither to control them nor passively sit back and criticize them. Maybe the people of Tahiti have the right idea: If someone shows affection toward their child, Tahitian parents will *give* the person their child. Many children there grow up without permanent parents, being passed on to adults who declare their admiration for them. Imagine being a kid raised by people who admire you!

Got my new IBM Selectric III typewriter today. A beauty. But I wonder if I'll actually get writing done. When Chrissie was here she'd sit with the girls, read them a story, and give me a chance to write. And that's another reason why I feel cheated by my two books: They were written at the expense of time I might have spent with Chrissie and the girls. How can I forget the tap on my door with Chrissie there with a cup of Sleepytime herbal tea for me? She put in honey and lemon; called it a "special brew."

The IBM salesman who brought the typewriter proved to be a blond, crew-cut, Joe Hardy type. Except for albinos, he was the whitest man I ever saw. He sat at the kitchen table excitedly telling me about his new baby, a daughter. We talked for an hour about typewriters and babies, then showed each other pictures of our children.

When he asked about my wife for the second time, I stupidly told him The Truth: my wife and oldest daughter had died.

At first he blinked and stared at me. Was I kidding? He looked so innocent, I don't think he'd ever met someone who had been constipated, never mind bereaved. Then his face dropped. Quickly he wrapped up the paperwork, thrust the warranty before me, and left, looking troubled.

I bet it was the first time he had ever entertained the idea that a wife and daughter could die. Not just a wife and daughter. Uh-uh. *His* wife and daughter. I felt sorry for him, but also a little irritated. As if *I* had upset his comfortable day. It's my fault. Should I have lied and told him Chrissie was out shopping? (Hey, sorry, Mr. Joe IBM! Don't worry! Your wife and baby look adorable, pink/white and blond like you. People like that don't die. Aw, I was just kidding! My woman's still around. She just kind of left me, y'know?) Nobody really knows loss—*knows it*—unless they've been through it. And if they have, then there is *no need for words*.

Music is a joy in my life. I spent one contented hour playing piano today. Years ago I would once in a while play hooky from school so I could spend the day in the cellar playing my old, beat-up, upright piano.

I taught myself to play. The only piano teacher I ever tried turned out to be a maniac: An elderly Italian with eyes like Mussolini, he was genteel and charming to my Mom, but turned into a mental case when we two were alone together for a lesson. He screamed insanely "No! No!" when I made a mistake, grabbing my chubby, stubby fingers, pressing them to the right keys.

After a few months, I began to use my two-bucks' piano-lesson money to buy *Superman* comics or a hot dog and orange drink at Nedick's at the corner of Church and Flatbush...

Today I enjoy playing piano for appreciative people. I have played at the local Mt. Ascutney Hospital in Windsor, and at senior citizens' days at nearby resorts. The elderly people love old songs; they sing along with any song I play. Seniors make the best audiences: They are so patient, and so grateful for anything you play. A few years ago I made the mistake of trying to earn extra money by playing piano at Vermont resorts. But most tourists are from the city, and city people think they own the world, especially the ones who drive up from Boston in their BMWs and Peugeots accompanied by brash children and brand new ski equipment. I'd rather be locked in a room full of life insurance salesmen than play piano for tourists.

A guy who had words like "Nike" or "Adidas" or "Puma" printed on absolutely every item of his clothing interrupted my pained rendition of "Killing Me Softly" to ask me if I knew something by Mantovani or 101 Strings.

Chrissie's sister Paula and niece Andrea finished their visit today—their first visit since the funeral. I drove them to the airport in West Lebanon today after going to the cemetery. As we walked back to our car after watching their jet disappear into the clouds, Aimee asked me if there was a phone number for heaven. She saw the phone number Aunt Paula jotted on a piece of paper at the airport... so Aimee wanted to call Mommy.

She talked about calling her mom as we drove home.

"Can we ask the operator for her number?" she asked.

I told Aimee there were no phones we could use to call Mom.

We're home. The girls are behind the house picking berries. They are feeling lonesome today for their mother. Katie looks mopey. God, I wish there was something—anything—I could do to make it better for them. What can I do?

Aimee has come back inside my office with a handful of wild blackberries, and she is eating them as she talks to me. Now she has just stuck her maroon finger in her ear. Her ear. Filthy! How could any woman want to be a full-time mother and homemaker? It's an impossible job. *Impossible.* I hate the idea that from now on, I'll have to check their ears, making sure they're clean. Chrissie used to do that (actually, she didn't mind doing it). I shudder to think about it and my anger is growing again.

I thought about the cemetery. Yesterday we went there for the first time since the burial. It was very difficult to be there— Even so, I felt it was important to go. The girls didn't seem to know what was happening. They wandered, picked wildflowers. It doesn't make much sense to them. Paula looked at the temporary little grave markers we placed there until we buy headstones. I couldn't bear to look at their names carved down on the ground: Olga, Paul, Christine Jean, and my baby Christine Anne. Names on the ground are painful as hell. On the ground, like dirt.

Aimee asked if we were going to get a headstone for Mommy's grave, and if so could we get a heart-shaped one? A special one, not like all the other ones. She wanted a smaller heart for Christine... I nodded yes to Aimee. I turned away. Kids can be so matter-of-fact. Looking at her, she seems not to be racked with pain. Thank God for that.

Thank God.

Thank you God for birds that sing, thank you God for everything.

I walked back to the car, not even seeing where I was going. It is impossible to believe my wife Chrissie, my little Christine, who had climbed trees and ridden her bike up and down the street, and my in-laws, Paul and Olga, who had sat and laughed at dinner with us, are, all of a sudden, there. Right *there*.

Déjà vu. Instantly, I felt the same desperate, empty feeling as in 1967 when my Dad was buried with full honors at the National Military Cemetery on Long Island. Dad was 47 when he died, but his life began ending many years earlier when he was poison-gassed and deafened and shellshocked at his stops in Italy and North Africa during World War II:

Sicily.

Monte Cassino.

Salerno.

Anzio.

Brooklyn.

12th floor, Veterans Administration Hospital.

National Military Cemetery, Long Island.

Thank you, God.

Thank you for the wonder of war.

As I got into the car I thought how I had lost four generations of my family. Grandpa Califano (who took over my bedroom when he moved in) died in his sleep in 1964. Less than three years later, my Dad died. And now in June 1980, I lose my wife and daughter. Grandpa was 84, Dad was 47, Chrissie was 31, and Christine was 6. A totally opposite progression from the way it usually is.

But deep down I know this: To blame God (or a god) is a cop-out; we kid ourselves when we do that. My father was gassed by people—men acting in fearful obedience to other powerful, male human beings who threatened to kill or hurt them if they did not kill or hurt people like my Dad. Likewise, my Dad was forced by powerful male human beings to kill or hurt people or be killed or hurt by them. War is as simple as that. To hold God (or a god) to blame, or worse, to say it is God's will—"God is on our side"—only justifies actions of those powerful male human beings who demand that other human beings kill and hurt people. To wage war in the name of God is the greatest act of cowardice possible: It allows someone to justify the mutilation of another human being and, at the same time, help the mutilator actually feel good about doing what God wants. "God" is a perfect excuse for tyranny by the cruel:

Thy will be done.

After the cemetery we went to Burger King. Maybe that is the new American religion: worshipping the Burger King. It's got everything: seats around the altar-like counters, the money collection, music, a King, a banquet—the whole thing!

I still keep the kitchen light on and the door unlocked every night, but reality is starting to creep in.

The sky is beautiful. I'm on my back, on the grass; the sky is framed by the white, clapboard house and an enormous sugar maple tree. I wish I could see past the blue of the sky. Past the apparent, the superficial. Chrissie could. She was wise for someone her age. She knew the importance of love. Giving, caring love. And that is what makes my emptiness so painful.

Chrissie, I need to see your face; touch your skin, the softness just for a minute, no a second. Come back. Not to me but to your kids. They miss your laughter and your touch.

Could I just hold your head against my chest? It hurts so much. Just sit next to me... here. I know you hear me, but can you see me?

Am I ever going to see you again?
And Christine? Please take care of our little girl. Hold her and hug her.

Here are Katie and Aimee with more flowers!
I feel you still with us. In me.

My quiet moments are filled with wishing and wondering. Right now I feel hopeful. I wish she could give me a sign she's "there" and everything is all right. She would if she could.
Like a little kid, I squeezed my eyes shut and talked to her.
"Please—PLEASE—tell me you're okay."
"Please—I miss you so much. I'm lonely."
"Chrissie, is there some way you can tell me you are at peace?"
Just as I opened my eyes, Katie and Aimee came running from behind the house, yelling, "Daddy, look at the flowers we picked for you!"
A bouquet of five daisies. Chrissie's very favorite flowers.

But where did they come from? The girls were playing behind the house, but behind the house are just berry briars and raspberry bushes. And besides, today is August 4. Daisies have been gone for a month or so.

She is with us.

Desperate this morning trying to get *them* dressed. Amazing. I can write a book called *Effective Parenting,* yet I cannot get a five-year-old child dressed!

I poured out Cheerios—a half-bowl each. It's a lot easier than cooking my special cheese omelets; Aimee calls them "smashed eggs." (She calls sunny-side-up eggs "flat eggs".) All three girls loved my sharp cheddar omelets, my Swiss and mushroom omelets—any omelets.

As milk drips off the table, it's boo-boo time:

"I've got a bug-bite on my foot... on my ankle... on my tush... on my ear..."

Naturally, all require a band-aid. On they go.

Off they come. We forgot Bactine.

On they go.

Off they come. They won't stick because of the Bactine.

And we are late for summer preschool.

I still make too much coffee in our (my?) Mr. Coffee coffee maker. Chrissie was concerned about the amount of coffee she drank. And her smoking worried her, especially when she was expecting. The government ought to mandate the same warning on cars as they do on packs of cigarettes:

"Warning: Travel in an automobile may be hazardous to your health. Automobile travel has been linked to sudden, unexpected death."

or, "Warning: Death is one, proven, potential side effect of travel in an automobile. There is rarely any warning, so be prepared for unexpected injury or fatality."

Aimee went to her friend's house today. I want her to adjust well. Perhaps little Katie will be oblivious, knowing of her mother only from pictures and from what I tell her. And she'll only know Christine and Grandma and Grandpa from me, and from home movies and photographs.

Katie does still cry for her mother. Instead of crying, Aimee asks many questions, which tells me this is her way of processing her grief.

How can I make things better for them? How can I relieve their pain? Can I?

Sometimes my longing and pain are powerful. I am sitting outside at the picnic table writing this. My pain is strong. I hear Chrissie in the living room talking and laughing with the girls as she watches TV. I hear her breathing at night as she sleeps. I see her hair, her eyes; I can feel her slender arms. I can smell her perfume; her soap; her body. Even though she weighs very little, I know exactly how far my body will drop when she gets into bed next to me.

> Chrissie, do you know what's going on here? Do you see me? You loved me so much while you were here, why can't you just… just come back into my life? I'm not asking for signals, or for a miracle, and I'm not asking you to prove your love to me by reappearing. You proved your love while you were here. I just miss you so much.
> You, and only you know how much I miss you. I wonder if you can see me. Can you laugh? Can you cry?
> I wish I hated you just a little. It would make things so much easier.

They are coming back toward me again: Aimee's screaming with delight over the berries, red and juicy. "No, stay away from those rotten ones." "Katie don't wipe your berry fingers on my pants!"

> Chrissie, these are *your* children. *Where are you?*

❧❧❧

The garden—untouched since their deaths—has literally gone to seed. With weeds six feet tall it looks like an abandoned lot in South Bronx. It had been a place of solace and peace. Now I tell my neighbors to help themselves, scrounge around and take whatever they find: There's a ton of vegetables under all the weeds: crooked, unthinned carrots, overly-large fibrous green beans, dried-out peas, immature, green pumpkins, tall, seedy lettuce, rotten tomatoes, and probably the largest killer zucchini ever raised lurks under all that brush.

I remember freezing time when the first produce was ready to pick. Usually, it would be peas. We'd blanch the vegetables, cool them, then race to the freezer with the full-but-dripping plastic bags. Although peas were eaten so fast they rarely made it to the freezer, we'd freeze gallons of green beans, corn, and carrots, and enjoy them in January as three feet of snow lay over our garden.

Aimee didn't want to go to Summer Bible School this morning; I didn't insist. She wanted to stay home and play with Katie, and that's fine. The girls will need to support each other throughout their lives; to be close and love each other when I'm gone.

Like any other self-respecting homemaker, I fight my boredom by going shopping. Aimee needed sneakers.

What the hell do I know about sneakers?

At Kmart I bought a bunch of things, including two, Rubbermaid, box-shaped organizers. These will help me sort out socks from underclothes.

Even though she's only two, Katie dresses herself completely, except for tying her shoelaces. And she comes pretty close! They need to be able to take care of themselves later in life. It starts now. Many American kids are too dependent upon parents to do everything for them from putting down lock buttons on car doors to picking up after them. No matter how well they do in school, American kids feel basically incompetent when they reach adolescence and adulthood. Parents are misguided when they try to do too much for their kids, try to give their kids everything they never had.

We had another "incident" today, this time at Kmart in Claremont. We were in the Kmart cafeteria, and as I moved a tray along the counter with my coffee and their root beers, a kindly looking, elderly cashier spoke with my talkative five-year-old:

"Hello. And what a pretty, white dress you have on! What's your name?"

Aimee took a step toward her and answered the question.

"Aimee?" she repeated, "What a pretty name! And is this your sister?" she asked, as I poured white chemicals into my coffee.

"Yes. Her name is Katie. But she doesn't talk much. And I have a big sister—her name is Christine...

I felt a knot in my stomach as I heard her name. Sensing what was coming next I tried to distract her.

"Aimee! Come here. Daddy needs help!"

But she was intent on her conversation.

"...Katie is two," she continued, "and Christine is seven... well, almost seven..."

"Two and seven?" the woman repeated.

"...yes, but she died. She was riding in my Mommy's car and..."

My heart fell. I looked into the coffee cup, put on a simple smile, and shrugged my shoulders. The cashier managed a weak, "Oh, dear!" and hurriedly rang up our order.

Aimee ran ahead to get two straws as Katie pulled on my jeans shorts, oblivious to everything but the thumb in her mouth.

I wanted to talk to Aimee about IT but I knew—I know—she's just too young. She wouldn't understand how we have to censor what we say. So I didn't say a word to her.

The ride home? Fine for a change. Thank God there was no "I want my Momma!" from Katie. I even put a Red Sox baseball game on the radio.

As we unpacked the car Aimee waxed ecstatic over her "clops" (as she called her new clogs). What a shopper's instinct. From seven identical Kmart bags on the floor, Aimee went straight to the bag holding her "clops."

The girls sacked out on the sofa. I made up two bottles of milk, put a clean diaper on Katie, reminded Aimee to brush her teeth, and went to open mail.

A statement from Vermont National Bank, junk mail to Chrissie, a postcard from my godmother Aunt Flora vacationing in Colorado, a postcard from Paul in Haiti (he came home twelve days ago—did the card come by rowboat?), and a small envelope addressed to "Mr. DiGuilio, Reading, Vermont." It looked like a local letter; a neighborhood child asked me to change my mind and be principal at Reading Elementary School.

I close my eyes at my desk and I see a truck coming at them. The truck that haunts me every time I drive; every time I lie down to sleep. I see that truck around every curve in the road, and it bears toward me, its rear end fishtailing, blocking both lanes of the two-lane highway.

Tonight—for the first time—I want to move far away from here. I want to go back to Brooklyn. I want to go to Connecticut, Florida, Canada, anywhere.

The house doesn't haunt me. I can handle constant reminders of my wife and daughter, but being near where they died is making my skin crawl. I can't sleep tonight as I write this. It's 1:25 a.m. right now.

The light above my typewriter is the only light on in the house.
It is so dark outside the window.
It is so dark inside the house.
I have never felt so alone in my life.

Today I finally read part of a book, *Up From Grief.* Very comforting ideas.

I had this dream last night. It's a scorching-hot day. I'm about to go and play tennis. Chrissie's there in her robe, not wanting to kiss me ("I have draaaa-gon mouth!"). I hear a voice—my little Christine calling "Maaaaaa!" from inside the house. I wave to Chrissie and drive away, but after a while I sense something is wrong and turn around and come home. They are all gone; the house is empty. I rush to the hospital. Everyone is standing along the sides of the road staring at me as I drive by. The hospital! I see a long white corridor. Chrissie is somewhere beyond the end of the corridor, perhaps behind a distant door. Intensive care unit. The doctors tell me maybe she'll pull through. Fifty-fifty chance. We'll know soon. "When?" I plead. They turn away, shaking their heads. "Soon," one mumbles as they go through shining, stainless steel doors. "Please tell me," I beg. "Please!"
Please.

Sometimes, something totally ridiculous happens that makes life bearable. At sundown I was driving north on the Connecticut Turnpike, heading out of New York City. Katie and Aimee were nodding off in the back seat. Somewhere beyond Bridgeport and, naturally, out of sight of any gas station, house, or other sign of civilization, there was a loud explosion.

Blowout. I pulled toward the side of the road, mounted the curb, and drove onto a flat, dirt shoulder. I was in the middle of nowhere.

Katie and Aimee were still in dreamland in the back seat. While they slept, I took out the jack, tire iron, and spare tire. I jacked up the car, and when I turned to get the spare leaning against a tree, it was gone.

Gone? Yes, gone.

Out of the corner of my eye I caught sight of it—rolling—far down the grassy embankment. Like an expert skier, it slalomed around each of two or three trees in its path.

"Run, run as fast as you can, you can't catch me, I'm the Michelin man!"

It disappeared into the twilight.

No phone in sight. It got dark quickly. I sat on the rim of the flat tire.

After an eternity (about fifteen minutes), a police cruiser came by and stopped. He walked over to examine my jacked-up car.

So glad to see the guy, I rattled on: "... and I got this blowout, see, and my kids are in the car. My spare tire rolled away like a shot..."

He offered to call a garage for help. As he walked to his cruiser, he asked about the girls and family. I rambled on about what had happened to me—my losing my wife and all.

He nodded, and leaned into his cruiser. Distracted, he scribbled something on his pad, then talked into the radio:

"I got a guy here with some problems."

"Go ahead. What's his problem?" asked a dispatcher's voice.

"His car died, and I think his wife just ran away."

He scratched his head and looked at me, "That's not right, is it?"

Who am I? Who was I? Who was I before I met Chrissie? When I was seventeen, who was I? I simply can't remember.

Death.

What do people say about death? "God wanted her"; "God wants all good people to be with him"; "Death is like sleeping"; "Only the good die young." I wish people could also say, "I don't know." We feel we must have an explanation/answer for everything, especially the one thing we know least about.

In Catholic school in the 1950s, I learned about death this way:

Class: "What happens, Sister Saint Susan, when somebody dies?"

Sister: "The soul leaves the body for the first of two judgments, called the 'Particular Judgment'. On your own, you are judged by Jesus, and the sentence is executed immediately."

There were four possible outcomes: Heaven (up) for the good, H—— (down) for the bad, Purgatory (sideways?) for the repentant, and Limbo (twilight zone?) for the unbaptized, aborted, and otherwise innocent non-believers.

As a child I had pictured the soul that leaves the body at death as being a clear plastic disc about five or six inches in diameter. It glowed, and lived somewhere around my heart, became darkened when I missed Sunday Mass, and would fly out of the body at the moment of death. According to Sister, the *only* question that was now unanswerable and unpredictable was whether it would fly up, or...—Sister's eyes darted back and forth—*down*. The direction depended upon how "dark" the soul was when the call came.

The nuns meant well I suppose, but they did not equip us to face real people dying. And because parents rarely took kids to funerals, death—like sex—remained a great mystery.

I have tried to be honest with Aimee and Katie. I have said, "I don't know," when I didn't know what to say. I have told them I don't believe death is the end of you; people are the great work of creation. We have the ability to love. To share love with humanity, with nature, and maybe most of all with another person. That loving/knowing of another is the thing that doesn't die. Call it a soul or whatever, that loving/knowing gives us a reason for living, and it gives a reason for dying. If there were no death, no living would be possible. The love I felt and still feel for Chrissie, for my little Christine, will never die. Nor will my love for my Dad, my grandparents, my in-laws, and all those other relatives and friends who were and are part of my life.

I made a list of "answers" to that hateful little three-letter word:
Q: Why? Why did they die?
A: Because they lived.

Q: Why did they live?
A: To share love. To know and be known by others.

Q: Why should I go on living?
A: Because if I don't live, and live now, and live well, then dying will have no meaning. Only life gives meaning to death.

Thirty-seven days now. A month, plus.

Today I finished the latch-hook rug Chrissie had been working on, but the crewel work escapes me.

It is fascinating how people in my town have been affected by the crash: Men started taking their wives out to dinner, people took time off work to take vacations they'd been putting off, began using seat belts, asked me where to get a will drawn up, and installed car seats for infants and toddlers. I'm glad it moved these people to do things. It's amazing how powerful a motivator is the fear of dying.

Today I started to pack up Chrissie's clothes. I put on music as I opened her dresser drawers. There were her blouses, sweaters, socks. I held her blouse to my face—it smelled clean, and a little like her powder. Placed them gently in clothing storage boxes. I decided to give them to Paula. She should have some of her sister's personal things. It also saves me having to decide what to do with things—keep them or part with them.

Why are shoes—her shoes—so difficult to face? They seem so much more personal than a blouse. I put the lid on the last box, and sat and cried for a half-hour, staring at her empty dresser and the empty spot under the bed where her slippers had been since That Day.

ða·ða·ða

As I tucked her into bed after reading her *The Cat in the Hat Comes Back,* Aimee asked me if people in Spain have cats.

"Spain? Yes, I think they do."

"But if people speak to cats in Spanish, how do cats understand?"

I had to think for a moment with that one.

ða·ða·ða

I have had that recurring dream several times: The one where it's a scorching-hot day, and I'm about to go and play tennis. Chrissie's always there in her robe, not wanting to kiss me ("I have "draaaa-gon mouth!"). I hear a voice—my little Christine calling "Maaaaaa!" from inside the house. I wave to Chrissie and start to drive away, but get sick and have to turn around. I drive back to the house. Chrissie is in her robe, pouring Special K into a bowl for Christine. Aimee is eating dry cereal, flake by flake from her bowl, and Katie is sitting on the floor with her Raggedy Ann doll. I hold Chrissie in my arms. "Please don't go today! *PLEASE* don't go." She shakes her head as if it's an impossible request and pours milk on Aimee's cereal. She looks at me and says, "I have to go." "No you don't!" I scream at her. "NO YOU GODDAMN DON'T HAVE TO GO!" She holds up her hand to me and says, "Don't worry. Things will be okay. You'll see. You always get nervous over nothing." And the dream just ends there.

I gave a workshop called "Hug 'Em or Slug 'Em: What's Your Teaching Style?" to a little over 100 teachers in a New Hampshire school district. They enjoyed it, and they learned something. Looking back over the time I spent preparing for it, I realized that when I am busiest I am happiest. Or at least, I am not feeling depressed. Same for Katie and Aimee. They never seem sad when they have things to do.

I have also been helping my replacement as school principal, supplying her with advice and ideas for her first school administration position. It feels strange being on the sidelines now that school's about to begin. A left-out feeling.

Two months have gone by. It doesn't hurt very much first thing in the morning. I wake up and it's, oh, yeah. A vacant feeling. The pain comes more in the afternoon, and mostly at night. Sunday is the worst day of the week; of any week. And nights are worst. Put them together, and you have Sunday night. I wonder if there are more suicides on Sunday and at night than other times?

Yes, I'm sure the numb stage is over. I feel an odd confusion now about many things that used to seem simple and be clear. Alternatives, choices, and decisions. Now it is hard to decide anything, and to tell what is real and what is imaginary. Did they really exist? If this unreal thing could have happened to them and to me, how could *anything* then be real?

That's it, and I mean it! No more Lucky Charms cereal in this house! Aimee and Katie have gotten up early every morning for the past few days and as they watched TV they picked out all the marshmallow bits—the clovers, diamonds, hearts, and the other, orange-colored objects—from the Lucky Charms cereal. Now they won't touch the remains. I liked the marshmallows, too. Not fair.

"Daddy, I'm hungry."

"Eat Lucky Charms."

"I can't! Katie picked out all the good stuff!"

"Sorry, can't help you."

"But I'm *hungry*, Dad!"

I pointed to the floor. "There's a piece of American cheese you left on the floor last night."

"That's yukky! You want me to eat something dirty off the floor?" She gave me what Grandma DiGiulio would call "the evil eye."

On cue, Katie walked by and left her footprint—à la Hollywood—on the slice of Kraft American. Aimee looked on in horror.

"Katie! That was my cheese! Daddy said I could have it... and you... you *stepped on it!*"

Katie looked at me, then down at the cheese. She peeled it off the floor; remarkably, it stayed intact as she held it out to Aimee.

"Gross! Katie, I can't eat that! You stepped on it!"

With a grin and a shrug, Katie ate it.

I had my first date. A blind date. I was like a thirteen-year-old, nervous and unsure how to act. "What if she doesn't like me?" "What if I call her Chrissie?" I just made believe that it was a person I was meeting—nothing special, nothing romantic—not a "date."

The hard part came at the end of dinner. The meal was wonderful, and we both felt comfortable talking. But when the check was paid and we were about to go, I asked myself What next? Should I take her home? Go somewhere for a drink?

I decided I would simply *ask her.* In the olden days, the man had to decide. Thank God those days are gone.

"What would you like to do?" I asked as I started my car.

"Oh, I don't know. I'm open for anything."

"Suggest something."

"Oh, I don't know. You decide." So much for modern times.

I then backed right into a car in the Grand Union supermarket parking lot. This was not easy to do, mainly because I was in the restaurant's parking lot at the time. The concrete barrier was missing, and as I was yakking about where we might go, I felt a jolt. It looked like a Mercedes. I hit it on its bumper and saw it rocking in my rearview mirror.

Things went downhill from there.

"Anything in particular you'd like to do?"

She stared at me. Doll's eyes. Absolutely vacant.

"Welllllll," she drawled, rubbing her chin.

(Inside I was feeling resentful—I don't need this. I was married and never had to be uncomfortable like this.)

We went for coffee; a nice place in Hanover called Peter Christian's Tavern. Then we drove to her house, and I gave her a hug. Big hug. But it felt wrong: She was, um, different, not the size I was used to. I think she understood. I hope she did. I kissed her cheek. She was nice, but not for me. Not the way I was now. Sorry. Perhaps I was the wrong person for her.

No wonder married people live longer than single people. Married people don't go out on dates.

I paid the sitter, put on a pot of Mr. Coffee. It is 1:00 a.m.

Thinking about my date tonight, I think I must be the "marrying type." I despise dating. To me, knowing someone is better than "the hunt." Trying to imagine what a woman *could* be comes too close to deciding what she *should* be. Because she is who she is. Would I want a woman to try to redesign me? Having an ideal woman is dangerous, because when you meet a real woman, your ideal will stand in the way of ever getting to know who that real woman is. I can *think* and *say* this, but I don't feel this way: Chrissie is my ideal woman.

But thank you, Chrissie, for giving me permission to date, to maybe love again. You were a wonderful wife and I miss you and will for the rest of my life.

Weirdness. After a talk I gave in upstate New York a couple of days ago, I was propositioned by, I think, a custodian or the UPS delivery man. When I collected evaluation sheets that participants filled out at the end of the workshop, I found a note asking me if I like sailing, for he had "a lovely sailboat," upon which he wanted me as his "special guest to sail Lake George." He thought me "charming"; best of all, he "adores burly men." Me, burly?

The anonymous writer had to be the skinny guy who had stood way in back, the one who seemed to laugh a little too loudly at my awful puns and jokes. I couldn't tell if he was a UPS delivery man on his way through the auditorium, or the school's janitor.

I thought about it. What would Chrissie say? "A guy? You replace me with a guy? Thanks a lot!"

I'm writing this in Meriden, Connecticut. Today we are visiting my sister Ann and brother-in-law Frank. And everything has gone wrong.

While I was out with Frank, Katie fell against a rocking

chair, split her upper lip and got a bloody nose. I took her to the emergency room at Memorial Hospital.

On the examining table, Katie played with a yellow bracelet they put on her wrist. As the nurse cleaned her upper lip, Katie asked to go home... and she started her "I want my Momma!" cry again.

The doctor came in; he examined her. To keep her occupied, he asked her questions about her Mommy. Idle chatter as he worked.

"Where's Mommy, hmmmmmmmmm?" he asked as he stooped to look at her lip. I tried to interject and soothe her.

"Daddy's here. Shhhhhh. Daddy's here."

The more Katie cried for her Mommy, the more he asked about her and the more Katie cried.

I took him aside and told him. Had to. He was torturing the kid.

Today is the first real day of autumn. Fall in Vermont is incredible. The leaves turn positively fluorescent in orange, red, yellow. The air smells woody, fresh, and crisp. Winter's air is sharp; fall's is crisp. Apples are for sale; a nearby orchard has them overflowing a roadside bushel basket. Tempting as you drive by. Pumpkins appear on wooden boxes in front of unpainted homes. It's time for a long walk in the woods, not just a hike to a summer swimming hole, nor a stroll to a secret old bottle-dig site in a forest glade. Take a few hours to walk in the woods. To hold hands and look; breathe in and with the forest.

I had no summer. I was numb in July and August and now that fall is here, I don't want to be cheated again. I want to enjoy something from 1980. After all, summer is gone but fall is here, and it is real Vermont. It's Chrissie and me raking leaves into huge piles four feet high (I smell them now!), and having the girls jump in. Christine and Aimee used to love to divebomb on top of the pile. Or, they'd slither into the massive pile and erupt out, a leafy volcano spewing lava. I have a home movie from last fall: Christine is standing with her leaf rake in front of a pile of leaves. Then all of a sudden, she's gone. Finally, Christine bursts out of the pile, shaking off leaves like a golden retriever fresh out of water.

Oh I miss my little girl so much. My heart aches for you, my dear daughter.

My "planned memories" are gone. Like a car that has run

out of gas, there are no more things for me to do that were part of us, decided by us, looked forward to by us. That is the strange silence of widowhood, of suddenly becoming unmarried. And it can feel terrifying. No one to talk with when you have been used to talking; even more, no one to plan to do things with when you have been used to doing so—these all cast a strange stillness on life. It goes beyond missing, beyond grieving. Words take on different nuances: talking, eating, sleeping, walking—all become transformed into new, but not novel or enjoyable experiences. The stillness of widowhood is not peaceful. It is alien. Perhaps "vacancy" is the best word to describe the feeling.

And irony is such an odd companion now. Driving through Vermont, I remember reasons why Chrissie and I moved here: We were both born and raised in New York City, but were not cut out to live there. We sought a peaceful pace, fewer people, and less conflict. We weren't "back to the land" types. Yet maybe we were heading that way, for Chrissie wanted to get one or two lambs ("as pets!" when she saw my mouth water at the mention of sweet, succulent lamb). Of course, I cherished our huge garden—I had joked with Chrissie about loving my tomatoes so much that I wanted to die falling amongst them the way Marlon Brando died in *The Godfather*. But with Chrissie's death, everything else also died. My garden died, the hope of having lambs died, making our life together died, and even my fancied death among my vegetables became coarse— now too close to reality instead of a mere jest.

We rode New York City's subways for years. And we came across the usual characters that scare non-natives: lost souls, loud street kids, flashers, and bogus nuns. We withstood two burglaries of our apartment, and several police investigations of murders in our Brooklyn neighborhood. As a teacher I routinely took away knives and fireworks, and once confiscated live ammunition from children in my inner-city public school. It seems ironic then to come to a placid land like Vermont and have my family decimated among pine trees and timid robins.

My feelings about being alone sometimes turn to resentment. For example, I filled out a questionnaire for a car insurance company. I checked yes next to the "married" box. I never left her. She never left me. We're not divorced. How can I be *un*married?

Can I be unmarried so easily? By a car crash? Yes, it's a

tragedy, but what has that to do with my marriage? *Our* marriage? Does the love we shared now end because society says we're no longer officially married?

It seems strange to hear the phrase I love him, or I love her. People say it all the time, but can one-way love be possible? Maybe we shouldn't allow the pronoun "I" to be used with the word "love." The only correct way to say it would be "*we* love." It would then only be possible for *both* to love. Each other.

Love used to be a special word. Years ago, teachers forbade us to use the word "love" when referring to inanimate objects or animals. You'd lose a point off your composition if you wrote "I love baseball" or "My dog loves me," for only humans were capable of love, and love was possible only between persons.

ঌ঺঺ঌ঺঺ঌ঺঺

In a way, I'm still locked in time; frozen into the end of June. School has begun, leaves are turning brilliant colors, but I'm still stuck in that hot, sweltering summer day when lightning struck. The day the state trooper called me to say... I don't want to remember.

Anger. Today I feel angry. I am enraged at Chrissie for leaving me. Angry as hell. Angry for her, too. She was cheated— she never got to see her violets blossom and grow; she never got to see her children grow. They were her happiness, and each thing or person that gave her joy now gives me grief. How curious that her happiness is now my sadness.

I think I am most angry for my children. She was more than a friend and a wife and lover to me. She was "Momma." Aimee and Katie miss her so much. Fair? They were cheated, both of them, so young. We still had Aimee's birthday cake in the refrigerator when I was dressing for the funeral. I feel that my anger is turning to bitterness.

And my little Christine was cheated too. But that's even tougher for me to think about. All I can do is close my eyes and rock her in my arms before I sleep at night and hope to kiss her cheek once again somewhere, someday. I have many words to describe the longing I feel for my wife, but I have no words to describe how I feel about my daughter.

My resentment has taken away my ambition, my desire to go to work; to contribute to society; to earn a living; to promote my book; to go for "the better things in life." Ha. Better things, indeed. How foolish are people who spend so much of their lives chasing flashy cars, fine jewelry, fancy college degrees, and neat, tailored green lawns. These are better things? Better than chronic diarrhea, I suppose.

Voilà, Snowball! Aimee's been asking for a kitten for so long. A pure white kitty. So we went to the Springfield Humane Society after calling 'round Vermont to locate a place that had a fluffy, white kitty. A gaunt attendant took us through the kennel area. Dogs barked and howled. Katie clung tightly to me and Aimee squeezed my hand and walked practically on my shoes.

"Is that where they punish bad dogs?" she asked, looking in horror at the snarling mongrels.

Ah, there are the cats, huddled at the far end of the kennel. I pointed out three white kitties, poking around a lethargic-looking mother.

"That's their father," said Aimee.

"How can you tell?" I asked.

"He looks very tired," she answered.

Aimee's eyes lit up with joy as she went right for a small, rat-like varmint. "Dad, I looooove her! Pleeeeeese let's get her!"

"She has fleas," said the attendant as she raised her apron to scratch both kneecaps at once.

Aimee wiggled her shoulders, "That's okay. We have flea collars."

"Wrap her up," said Dad, scratching his head.

"She needs more'n a collar, Sweetie," the attendant said.

After promising to dust "Snowball" with flea powder when we got home, we packed her into the cardboard box with holes carefully cut out.

Aimee had written "SNOWBALL" on the box, complete with the backwards "N" just like in old *Our Gang* comedies. The only problem was our dear cat, Thelma. Thelma is a fat ,old, crusty tomcat whose original owner was uncertain or uncaring about the cat's gender. He called the cat "Selma," but with his lisp it was "Thelma." Anyway, Thelma swatted the intruder Snowball, and I had to separate them to prevent murder.

Aimee, however, was delighted. She thanked me over and over. Katie patted the cat and said, "Hi, 'no-balls."

I'm glad for Aimee, but I'm concerned that depression is setting in for me. I've sat at the kitchen table for long periods of time this past week, wondering if I made a mistake by giving up my school principal's job. I have never before in my life felt depressed, but now I know how bad it feels. I feel so gloomy; just don't want to do anything. I don't want to get dressed, bathe, shave, or do anything. Going out to get Snowball helped; it was something to do.

Today I perked up. I feel somewhat jubilant today. Why? My sister called to invite the girls to Connecticut, and thereby give me one weekend of freedom. I promised Aimee I'd take care of Snowball, and as I drove them to Connecticut I mentally explored what I might do. Maybe call my doll-eyed date. Wait— wait—wait! What about that congenial waitress at Howard Johnson's in Boston? My waitress! I've thought about her; how she leaned toward me, smiling at me. Her sharp but gentle, soft brown eyes, mellifluous cheeks. She didn't have to smile at me; she wanted to smile at me.

> When I closed my eyes she was near me, wanting me and gently kissing me on my neck… and when she spoke she was whispering, "Bob, I love you."
> "No, no… not yet," I'd protest.
> "But I can't lie; I can't help it. And the worst part is I need you so badly."

I have to go back to Boston. Must find out about her, and right away, because you never know how long waitresses stay on at places like HoJo.

Sunday's free. I'm going on Sunday to see her, and wait till her shift is over to take her out. When I think of her, I feel hopeful and a little cheerful. And excited.

At 12:15 this morning I got back from Connecticut. Thelma was curled up on the sofa; he looked peeved at having to wear a flea collar! I turned on the bath water and sat at the piano. As my bath filled, I played Scott Joplin tunes. My favorite is "Sunflower Slow Drag," written around 1899. Joplin was a genius, but a forgotten one: His grave was unmarked until

1973, and only because of the success of a movie (*The Sting*) that featured his piano music.

Took the hottest bath possible (Is that an anti-depressant!) and did a cakewalk naked and steaming into the laundry room to get clean clothes.

I saw Snowball sprawled on the rug.

I touched her. She was cold.

Terrified, I held my fingers to her side trying to feel breathing, a heartbeat, anything.

Nothing. Wait, something. She cried. Only a weak cry; her mouth remained open.

I yelled at her: "Damn. Wake up stupid cat!" Feeling like an ass, I sat naked and petted her, and warmed a bowl of milk and pushed it near her, covered her with a doll's blanket and turned on an electric space heater. Sitting on the linoleum, I was crying for this dumb cat.

After a half-hour I tip-toed back to Snowball. She had moved! I picked her up and brought her upstairs. Defying my grandmother's warnings ("Never sleep with a cat—it'll take your breath away!"), I laid Snowball on the pillow next to mine. I prayed for her to live.

My prayer may as well have been a Kaddish. In the morning Snowball was ice cold; her body thick like clay. Damn. I started to get mad again. Just what Aimee and Katie need. But wait, there was hope: The two other kittens at the Humane Society! I called, but the attendant told me all her cats had been impounded because "something killing the cats was going around."

Panic. I took out the *Yellow Pages* and called every Vermont and New Hampshire humane society in the directory.

"Hello? I'm looking for a white kitten. Yes, white. Oh? No, but thanks anyway."

Not one white kitten in six counties of New Hampshire and Vermont? All morning, I called pet stores, veterinarians, animal shelters, and even a couple of dairy farms. I found one—a farmer in Henniker, New Hampshire, thought his wife might part with a white kitten; she had three. I called her phone number (were they divorced?), and—talk about connections—when I mentioned her husband's name as the source of her number, she snarled, "definitely not," and hung up.

Desperate. I thought about getting a nonwhite kitten and concocting a fabulous tale that we had a rare and amazing chameleon, color-changing cat. But reason prevailed.

I wound up going back to the Springfield Humane Society and begging: Could I *please* have a white kitten if I *promise* to take it *directly* to a veterinarian to be checked out?

The attendant pushed back her sleeve and scratched her arm. Then she agreed.

I took *both* remaining white kittens. I'll tell Aimee Snowball got lonely for his brother.

They were teeming with fleas. When the box was opened on the vet's examining table, hundreds of fleas lay at the bottom of the box. Fiercely I scratched at my thigh, my elbow. My butt itched ferociously.

But Snowball II and III seemed just fine.

I woke up early and buried Snowball I. In a deep hole out by the old tamarack tree. And I burned her bedding, box, and the home Aimee and Katie made for her out of a Pampers box.

Aimee comes home with Katie tomorrow. I hope she can't tell that neither Snowball II nor III is the real Snowball.

After the burial, I drove to Boston to Howard Johnson's. No sign of my waitress. I sat at the counter. A large black woman wiped the counter. After I ordered, I tried to engage her in conversation.

"Uh, is there a waitress who works here... she's got brown eyes, roundish face, and..."

"White girl?" she asked.

I nodded. She looked a little suspicious.

"Why? You after her or something?"

My elbow slipped off the counter.

"No, just wondering. She had brown eyes... was real nice to me a couple of months ago and I forgot her name and was just wondering..."

"Liane. You talkin' 'bout Liane?" she asked.

Liane. Liane DiGiulio. Mrs. Liane DiGiulio. Liane and Bob. L & B. Love and Beauty. Looks and Brains. Lithe and Buxom. Lips and...

"I, uh, think so. Yeah. That's it."

"Well, she don' work here no more. She be at 'Custis'."

"Custis?" I asked.

"C-U-S-T-E-R-S" she spelled. "Cus-tis." "Issa place downtown," she said.

I thought for a moment to look for Custer's, but chickened out. Had to get on my way to Connecticut. Besides, the saying goes, Be careful of what you wish for—you may get it. What would I do if I found Liane?

≈≈≈≈

Why are Jesse Helms and Ronald Reagan (who will slaughter Carter in next month's election) spending so much time yelling about school prayer? There are so many other important issues facing our society. We already have freedom to attend any religious or non-religious schools we want; we already have freedom to have our own children pray all day if we so choose. Why is it so important to impose prayer on other people's children? On other people's families? On our public schools? And who will decide which prayers to say? Who will lead the prayers? Here's a better issue for you, Senator Helms. Auto and truck crashes kill fifty thousand people a year.

How about raising the driving age to twenty-one?

How about providing mandatory detention—jail—for those convicted of driving while impaired? Driving dangerously?

How about putting speed governors on all trucks? School buses used to have them: They are special gears put on the drive shaft of the bus that simply does not allow the axle to turn faster than a preset rate of speed. If you've driven on the Connecticut or New Jersey (or any) Turnpike, you know what it's like when a double-wide tractor trailer storms by at 75 miles per hour, or tailgates you three feet behind your rear bumper. Will our politicians ever face the fact that cars and trucks are lethal weapons? They go on and on about gun control: Yes, guns cause ten thousand deaths, but most of them are accurately called "murder." Motor vehicles? Fifty thousand deaths, all of them are called "accidents." It is much easier for politicians to raise and ride on controversial issues (like school prayer) to distract us from the realization that little of real substance can be accomplished through legislation.

Wrong word "accidents." Getting hit by lightning is an accident. Being killed by a drunk driver is not.

There are many other ways we can cut deaths. The problem is that they are not so obvious. For example, we might save a hundred deaths and injuries each year by simply installing clocks in shopping malls. Have you noticed that there is no clock anywhere in any shopping mall in America? Why? To keep people stone-blind to the time of day so they stay longer than they intended. The longer people stay the more they will spend. But how many people—once they are outside and realize the time when they get into their cars—how many people tend to race out of the parking lot? There was a terrible crash at a Connecticut shopping mall last week. The driver who caused the crash had overstayed at the mall and was practically flying out of the huge parking lot.

I am hurting again today. I played Scrabble with a friend, and when I opened the box, there was the score pad from the last game I played. With Chrissie on June 25, the night before she died. We stayed up together late that night to talk, to be together. She kept score. I had won by twelve points. But only—she had reminded me—because I had gotten a seven-letter, fifty-point word in the game!

"You're incredible! So lucky!" she said.

Next to my total she wrote the word "Lucky" with an arrow to my name. She had her robe on; her faded blue robe. Her hair was cut short and curled in little semicircles.

I look at the Scrabble score paper and get a creepy feeling: Did I have any idea of what would happen the next morning?

Sure. Chrissie, the girls, and my in-laws were going to Stoughton Pond, and I was going to Woodstock to play tennis.

Did I know—should I have known—that in less than twelve hours my wife, daughter, and in-laws would be dead? As I sat at the kitchen table with Chrissie at precisely 10:55 p.m. that night, was there a sign? As she brushed her teeth; as we got into bed; as I kissed her good night; as she went to the girls to check on them... should I have seen? Seen that that night was the last time I'd ever hug her in bed; the last time ever I'd hold my wife?

Snowball II is not doing well. Bad case of diarrhea. My friend came over with Kaopectate for cats, and yogurt. We shot the stuff into Snowball's mouth.

Aimee (who still thinks Snowball II is Snowball I) has changed Snowball II's name to "Blueberry," and Snowball III is now "Crazy Boy." (Katie still calls each cat "'no-balls.")

The girls are in bed as I write this. And I'm glad, because Blueberry is on the kitchen floor and she's convulsing. Not much more I can do for her. I'm sick of this crap.

At around 6:30, Aimee got up and came downstairs. Katie trailed behind her.

The Question, of course.

"Where's Blueberry?"

I told Aimee that Blueberry was pretty sick.

"I stayed up with her almost all night, Aimee, but she died this morning."

The Look.

The same look Aimee had at the hospital. Her eyes opened wide—she seemed to feel both terrified and disbelieving.

"Really, Dad? Are you joking? Is Blueberry (Mommy, Christine, Grandma, Grandpa) really dead? Tell me the truth!"

"I am, Hon."

Katie slowly shook her head, "Poor 'no-balls."

"Is Crazy Boy going to die, too?" asked Aimee.

I look at the last surviving white kitten, very alive, so spunky yet ratty, swatting a doll's shoe around the kitchen floor.

"No way! Crazy Boy looks fine."

Aimee wiped away her tear.

"I think so too, Dad. God's got too many kittens already— He doesn't need another one right now."

I want to smile, but she said it so seriously, all I can do is hug her.

After school, Aimee went with Katie and me out to the far garden near the apple trees. We dug a deep hole. As the girls gathered flowers, I took the cat out of the box and wrapped her with cloth—didn't want to see dirt being tossed on her. We pushed dirt in and as Aimee cried, she put little wildflowers and a few of Chrissie's purple alyssum on the patted soil.

Katie said, "G'bye 'no-balls."

Aimee went back out to show Blueberry's grave to her friends; they all picked scads of flowers and sprinkled them on the ground.

Good grief. Now Crazy Boy has diarrhea. A soap opera, my life.

If it's a virus, he'll probably die. If bacterial, there's hope.

Aimee, who I've decided is tougher than I, asked: "Dad, if Crazy Boy dies can we get another kitten?"

(Swell. Just what I need.)

"Sure. But we'll be sure to get one that's definitely healthy, right?"

She shrugged.

"Dad, *somebody's* got to take care of all these defective cats!"

Today's Chrissie's birthday. She would have been thirty-one.

 za·za·za

Florida. We're headed for Florida to visit friends and spend a day each in Disney World, Sea World, and Circus World. I'm writing this on the train right now—it's difficult to write on a train. Should have brought a typewriter.

We are now sitting in Amtrak's Club Car, which is filled with cigarette smoke. Ghastly. Otherwise, I'm in bliss, looking forward to a fun trip to sunny Florida. I love trains. It takes about 24 hours one-way to Kissimmee, but the advantages are great: no phones, nothing to worry about, time to nap, read, watch the world go by.

I got into a card game with three guys: a forlorn Navajo soul headed for Key West, a blonde crew-cut soldier headed for Quantico, and a chain-smoking guy from New Jersey who is a dead ringer for Dom DeLuise. I sat Aimee and Katie in the booth directly behind mine so I could drink my coffee and play cards. No, girls, no goodies... We'll have dinner in about a half-hour.

Lost in my poker games, I turned to check on them. As if by magic, their table was filled with goodies: cupcakes, Milky Way bars, and cans of soda. I asked them where all the stuff came from. As usual, Katie had a chocolate ring around her mouth.

Katie pointed and said, "Her." Aimee clarified:

"Dad, that really nice, dark lady bought us all this stuff."

Right on cue, a huge black woman squeezed out of her booth and came over. She was so big Katie could have tap danced atop her breasts. She told me how precious Katie and Aimee were, and what a "fine father" I was, and how she hoped I didn't mind her getting the girls sweets. I thanked her for treating the girls, but didn't have the heart to complain, "And thanks for ruining their dinner."

When she left, Aimee cleared up the mystery for me.

"She asked if our parents would mind if we had a soda, and I told her there was nobody to ask, because our Dad was busy gambling and our Mom was dead. Then she picked up Katie and started crying. And then she went and bought us all this stuff! Dark people sure are nice! You want some?"

za·za·za

My depression is not as continuous; I don't sit for hours; I don't stare out the window. When I do things, I feel better. Taking that first step, however, is still the hardest part. I don't know if this is bad or good, but today was also the first time I consciously thought back on what happened That Day:

I recall I was reading *The Words* by Jean-Paul Sartre at 11:00 a.m. on June 26. I left tennis at around 10:30 a.m., and headed toward Bridgewater to the school superintendent's office. I stopped at a snack bar in Woodstock at 11:00. I ordered a chickenburger and coffee, and as I waited I sat at a picnic table and read. Hadn't read Sartre since 1970 when Chrissie and I were in the same philosophy course at St. John's University. The burger was ready at 11:05 (I kept impatiently looking at my watch), and I read to page twelve. Sartre was talking about death... on page nine, he spoke of his mother's death: "Dying isn't everything: one must die in time..." It was getting too depressing. At 11:10, I closed the book and ate the burger. I headed toward the office of the superintendent of schools to find out how much money my school could spend on books. Good. Everyone's gone to lunch—I could get something done.

I was alone in the office when the phone rang:

"Hello, this is the Vermont State Police. We need to locate a Robert—uh—DiGiulio."

He pronounced it with a hard g.

"DiGiulio. This is he speaking."

Police? Me? I froze.

"Mister DiGiulio..."

"What's wrong, Officer?" I interrupted.

My voice shook. He took a deep breath and again identified himself.

Something was wrong; I interrupted him again, needing instant reassurance.

"My wife. Is my wife okay? What happened? My baby? Tell me!"

"Mister DiGiulio, I need to talk with you in person and..."

He wouldn't reassure me. Something was very wrong. Tears came to my eyes; I wiped them off and wiped off my glasses. My chest hurt.

"Please, Officer! Please tell me: Are they all right? Did something happen to my wife? My baby?"

"Look, Mister DiGiulio..."

"Please stop calling me Mister DiGiulio for God's sake!"

He was even-voiced, patient, and still formal.

"Mister DiGiulio, where are you now?"

"At the school superintendent's office on Route 4 in Bridgewater."

I couldn't find a chair; I sat on the floor. I pulled the phone off the desk; it crashed to the floor. He told me to stay put and he'd send a cruiser to pick me up.

"Officer, please. I can't wait here... I can't!"

"Sir, our cruiser is on its way to you. Stay there."

I hung up and desperately tried to call two friends; I kept mixing the digits of their phone numbers. No luck. I called my home. No answer. Nothing. I was panicking; I packed my briefcase and flew toward the door. The phone rang. I flew back to it. (Please God, let it be the police saying it was a mistake!)

"Good afternoon. I'd like to speak with the director of special education. This is the State Education Department..."

"What—?"

"This is the State Education Department..."

It made no sense. How could they? Who? I dropped the phone and ran out the door. Incredible heat crashed against me. There—my car is there. Threw briefcase through open window into back seat. Got in. Lit cigarette. Got out of the car and ran out onto U.S. Route 4. Desperate. Nothing. No police cars coming.

Ran back to my car. Two lit cigarettes in ashtray. I began to bargain with God. Pulled out onto Route 4. A car almost hit me. I drove toward Bethel, burning my eyes through the windshield for a police cruiser heading toward me.

(Hold it. It could be anything! Chrissie isn't dead! How stupid! She's been injured and they decided not to tell her parents. After all, I'm her husband, and they always tell the husband, not the parents.)

Cars seemed to go by me like blurs. I crushed out one of the cigarettes.

(Or what really happened was the house burned down, and they can't reach Chrissie because she's at Stoughton Pond! The telephone will sound to a caller like it's ringing, even though it's been... disconnected... or melted... by the heat?)

It's 1:15 P.M. No police car coming. Can't think.

Something's wrong.

I knew she was not alive.

 za za za

Married people probably don't realize how protected they are, insulated from the chaotic world of people looking for love. My very first perception of being newly single is this:

People are obsessed with sex. For example, I resent pressure to prove myself to be "straight." As I danced with a woman at the Sheraton, she told me "All the attractive men a woman meets today are either married or gay."

Annoyed that I was forced to deny I was either, I asked her, "What's wrong with being married or gay?"

She looked at me as if I had two heads (or was married or gay, or both) and said:

"They're both unavailable and don't want to get involved. They are dead-ends."

"But," I asked, "isn't who a person is more important than the category you decide to fit him into?"

She did not take this well.

"Would you," she stormed as she stepped on my foot, "want to go out with a gay woman? Hmmm?"

"If I enjoyed being with her and she with me, why not?"

She squinted at me.

"Boy, have you got a lot to learn! Wait till you're my age and still single and see if you don't think differently!"

Damn this sex business. I didn't have to prove anything to Chrissie. That's probably why I enjoy being with married women. They're "safe," plus I have a lot in common now with my married, homemaker, women friends: We talk detergent—how Wisk is on sale at Grand Union for $1.79; how long to defrost a roast beef; how to use "time out" when kids have been fighting.

As I get older I find I have less and less in common with men. What men do I know who understand what it's like to try to put a supper together that everyone will like? Men should be required to spend time not in military service but in domestic service.

The girls are in the living room and they're playing with toy telephones.

Aimee sounds joyous.

"Katie, Momma's on the phone! She wants to talk to you!"

Electrified, Katie runs over and grabs Aimee's play phone.

"Hello, Momma?!" She looks at Aimee, open-mouthed.

"Katie, Momma's at the hospital having another baby. You can't talk too long." She grabs the phone from Katie.

"A girl? You had a girl! You see, Katie? Mom had a girl! We have a new sister!"

Aimee turned her back to me; she noticed I was eavesdropping.

She spoke—sotto voce—into the phone:

"When are you coming home from the hospital, Momma? Yes, I miss you very much."

A pause.

"Mom, Katie's been very, very good. She's learned how to talk, and now she won't shut up! Hurry home. All of us are waiting for you."

I have to turn off the typewriter and give them a bath.

They're now in bed, and as I looked at their play phone left on the floor, my thoughts went back to the police calling me. How I flung down the office phone, flew into my car and was driving ahead, searching for the police car coming to meet me. I saw it.

> The police cruiser! The car was coming toward me; I flashed my lights and blew the horn, waved my arm out the window. They slowed to view this unknown maniac; I screamed my name at him. He nodded and motioned me to pull over. I drove my Rabbit onto someone's lawn, watching him desperately in my rear view mirror. Tore out of the car and dashed back across Route 4. He told me to get into his police cruiser. I got in.
>
> "No! Please don't tell me. No! Please don't—no!"
>
> Like a child creating noise to block out painful words, I held my hands to my ears and spewed out refusals. He began to speak, but I watched his mouth, matching the pitch of my crying to the moving of his lips. He tried to talk above my noise.
>
> "Mister DiGiulio, it is my duty to tell you..."
>
> "Nooo!" I grabbed his right arm. He resisted; I almost pulled it out of its socket. I apologized, then did it again.
>
> "I'm sorry. Look... please don't say anything. Just give me a few seconds. A cigarette. Do you have any?"
>
> He gave me neither time nor cigarettes. I looked at his eyes as he shifted his gaze from the windshield to me. He swallowed.
>
> "Mister DiGiulio, there was an accident this morning in Weathersfield..."
>
> "No! Please don't tell me. My wife, my baby..."
>
> "It is my *duty* to tell you..."
>
> "Well, I don't care! I DON'T WANT TO KNOW!"

"...and your wife..."

"STOP! I DON'T WANT TO HEAR THIS!"

"...and your six-year-old daughter were killed this morning in Weathersfield."

I tried to get away, out of the cruiser. Couldn't see anything but groped for the handle. He put his arm across to restrain me. He told me he was sorry. I sat and cried.

⁂

All the mothers and I are meeting tonight to escort our kids around the village for trick-or-treating. Aimee is a nurse; Katie's going to be a store-bought Bullwinkle the Moose, and I'm a father masquerading as a mother. As I dressed her, Aimee's face darkened, deep in thought.

"Daddy," she asked, "when I get married, would you help me pick out a wedding gown?"

A wedding gown?

"Sure! But only if you promise to let me pick a chocolate bar from your trick-or-treat bag, yes."

She laughed. "Okay. It's a deal! But don't eat everything!"

A wedding gown?

⁂

This morning Aimee summed up parenthood: "Being a Mommy is the same as being a Daddy except you have kids."

⁂

I thought of Liane. At Custer's in Boston. I called directory assistance and got their phone number. I need excitement.

Dialed Custer's... no answer. Will try again.

Another strange-but-true tale: Upon being asked to do a workshop for single parents in Springfield, I wrote to Parents Without Partners to get some up-to-date resources to pass along at the end of my workshop.

They sent me a packet, including a sample copy of the magazine *The Single Parent*, a list of P.W.P. chapters, and a photocopy of the index page and title page of a new book for single parents called *Single Through Death* circled; the word "recommended!" had been penciled in.

The book was *When You Are a Single Parent*.

It looked familiar.

I wrote that book.

Sometimes you gotta laugh at life.

Found out I have to be appointed guardian of my Katie and Aimee by the Court. Are they serious? A natural father—"guardian?" Of his two children? Who the hell do they think they are?

It's been five months short one day. Looking back, I see my life is now more on an even keel—I don't feel the burning anger I felt last month, nor do I feel numb. Kind of .blah, vacant. As I drove back from Purity Supreme supermarket in New Hampshire (no sales tax there), my mind went to my ride in the police car, right after the police trooper told me.

> We drove away; he said nothing more. The radio crackled. I apologized profusely for my behavior. He nodded.
>
> "My baby. And my Aimee. Where are they?"
>
> I was prepared to hear anything now; I hoped I had someone left to be with.
>
> "The baby was in the car. She's in Springfield Hospital. We're going there right now."
>
> I felt a wave of nausea.
>
> "Is she in intensive care? What about Aimee?"
>
> "The baby is alive. But that's all I know."
>
> "But Aimee! I have three daughters! Where's Aimee?!"
>
> "Mister DiGiulio..."
>
> "Dammit, call me Bob," I demanded, irritated and sick.
>
> "Bob, I don't know where she is. I'll radio ahead, but we only found two children at the accident."
>
> My head was throbbing. Aimee had been thrown, I knew, into the woods somewhere. He spoke mumbo jumbo into his radio; a crackling woman's voice responded. I couldn't decipher a single word.
>
> "Your daughter—the baby—is not badly injured. She's not in intensive care. We'll be there soon."
>
> Our police cruiser was met by another. They led me by hand from one police car to another. Like a trained bear, I followed. I asked the new officer about Aimee as we drove away.
>
> "She's fine," he answered. I searched his face for signs of lying.
>
> "She's at a neighbor's house," he continued, "and she wasn't in your wife's car. She was with a neighbor."
>
> I nodded dumbly. I recognized the neighbor's name he recited.

I saw barricades ahead. The highway was closed. He turned left in detour. Before I could get the words out, he nodded, yes, that's where it happened.

Past the barricades I could see nothing but more road.

I asked if he had a cigarette; he gave me a pack from his visor. I asked about my in-laws.

"...my mother-in-law and father-in-law are up to see us from New York City..."

I put my head in my hands.

"...and I don't know how to tell them. My wife—their daughter—and Christine is..."

He looked stricken. He placed his hand on my kneecap.

"Bob," he spoke in a kind but uncertain voice, "your in-laws were in the car."

And it became a crummy movie. This can't be real. I stared out the window. I knew the answer before I asked the question.

"Are they alive?"

He looked at me quickly, then straight ahead. He shook his head, slowly.

"No, they didn't make it. Sorry."

≈≈≈

I dated my doll-eyed woman again. I kind of like her but I dream of Liane. My Liane whose large brown eyes are searching for me somewhere in Boston.

Anyway, "Dolly" and I went to see a Rodney Dangerfield film called *Caddyshack;* it was funny and absurd. Afterwards, Dolly sat at my kitchen table as I cooked up fresh broccoli with a light homemade cheese sauce, chicken parmigiana, and had a nifty wine and glistening salad to go with it all. Whenever my mama made chicken or veal parmigiana and people raved, she'd turn to us kids and whisper, "Parmigiana is the easiest dish in the world to make!" She's absolutely right. Seeming both impressed and quite famished, Dolly looked at me as I stood at the stove.

"Bob," she said, "You'd make someone a hell of a wife!"

I took it as a compliment. She means I'm a "giver," someone who likes to take care of people. It's too bad that this is still mostly a woman's role. Men miss out on giving, nurturing, feeding, caring, dreaming. Why are these still the province of women? Why do so many men settle for so little?

I cannot think of a more lonesome existence than that of a

man who spends the greater part of his day with people he competes with and usually dislikes, only to come home and spend his remaining moments too tired to be with those who love him most. Because of circumstance, I have been more lonely and solitary these past months than I ever imagined. But why would someone *choose* to be lonely and solitary?

❧❧❧❧

The snow is falling, and it's absolutely gorgeous. A magnificent quiet outside as snow whispers itself onto the ground. Silent, snowy Vermont; snow makes the peace profound. Déjà vu. I felt this way—hushed and awed—many years ago as I sat with my dad at 6:00 a.m. Sunday Mass in our cathedral-like, parish church, the Immaculate Heart of Mary.

For the first time in a long time, Kate began asking for her momma again as I sat at my desk typing notes for tomorrow's lecture in Claremont. I picked her up, and she sucked her thumb, laying her head against mine. Yet, she does not seem unhappy. When I hold her she stops saying, "I want my Momma," and perks up.

Aimee on the other hand, says nothing. But I know she's also hurting. She keeps asking about getting a Christmas tree, but I just don't feel like getting one. For the past few years, we'd all pile into the car and go deep into the woods in South Reading, along an old logging road, select a little balsam or spruce for our low-ceilinged living room, tie it on the car roof, and drive home peering through a windshield being clawed by wild branches.

When I suggested we go to Aunt Ann's for Christmas, she seemed satisfied.

As I type this, the news is on. Dear God. A fellow from Honolulu shot John Lennon last night on a New York City street. Why would somebody want to shoot John Lennon? I worry for us; for our children. We haven't come far since the Stone Age. When somebody asked Mohandas Gandhi, "What do you think of Western civilization?" he replied, "It would be a good idea."

❧❧❧❧

Christmas Eve. We're in Connecticut with Ann and Frank. They have a real tree (for the first time). Everyone's trying, I think, to make just a little more noise to help banish the scary silence. I miss them so much tonight, but I won't show my sister how unhappy I feel.

Driving to Connecticut I turned to see Aimee and Katie fast asleep in the back seat. Out of fear, I wanted to grab them and put them next to me. The back seat is too far; I am afraid they will fall out or will disappear. I laughed at myself when I realized I had adjusted the inside rearview mirror to see not on my rear window, but my two daughters sleeping in the back seat.

As I drove I realized that my mind was wandering back to when I had seen them at the hospital six months ago:

The hospital. The trooper leads me in. I'm desperate to see my daughters. Katie. Aimee. People in white give me water and pills. I sit down; I stand up. There's my friend. Was it a big truck that hit them? Are these people all lying to me? They take me upstairs. In a room. Katie. KATIE! She is in a clear plastic crib; part of her head is shaved. A spot of blood.

I pick her up. *I will never let her out of my arms again!* Someone keeps telling me Aimee is alive, too, and will soon be here. I ask when. Right away, a few more minutes. I can't stand up when I try. Katie's face is pressed against my neck. She looks at me and softly says "Dada." She has purple welts. They make a V from shoulder to abdomen to shoulder. Her cheek is bandaged, as is her right arm. She is alive. All right. I won't let go of her; I sit on a cot with her against my chest. It's my fault because I let go of them. I won't let go again. I swear they will have to kill me, too, to make me let go again.

The door opens and Aimee walks in. I am relieved again. Anne and Neil brought her to me.

"Hi, Dad! What are we doing here?"

She is puzzled as she walks around the cot and kisses me. Her eyes grow large as she sees Katie in my arms.

"What happened to Katie?"

I can hardly speak—I whisper, "She's okay."

"Where's everybody? Where's Mommy? Where's Christine?"

All I can do is swallow. I lay Katie down on the cot and have Aimee put her head against my shoulder.

"Aimee, Mommy and Christine..."

I can't continue. She tilts her head, puzzled.

"Mommy and Christine... they died. They—"
She sat up and stared at me.
"For real, Daddy? Please don't joke."
"For real. Oh, I *wish* it were a joke."
She cried—a strange, long, loud wail."
"No, Daddy, *don't joke!* Mommy said she wasn't going
to die for a long, long time!"
She put her thumb in her mouth and lay back on
the cot. She sat up suddenly.
"When are we going home? I hate this place. Will
Grandma be my new mother now?"
On the back of the hospital room door is a poster of
a warm rural scene and poetry—poetry I remember from
Catholic school many years ago. Part of an excerpt I
had to memorize, by our "fourth-grade poet," James
Russell Lowell:

And what is so rare as a day in June?
Then, if ever, come perfect days;
Then Heaven tries earth if it be in tune,
And over it softly her warm ear lays...

ɘ.ɘ.ɘ

Christmas Day. Too many gifts! Aimee is knee-deep in gifts
asking, "Is that all? Where are the rest of them?"
Katie is joyful; she's jumping from toy to toy, excitedly
trying things out.
"Ohhhhh! Just what I always wanted! T'ank you, Dad! T'ank
you, Aunt Ann and Uncle Frank!" I had never seen Katie so
overjoyed.
And right there, my heart lightened up. I went into the
bathroom and just sat on the toilet seat and cried because
Katie finally looked happy.

ɘ.ɘ.ɘ

Aimee has been asking me if she'll need shots... inoculations.
She's afraid of shots.
"They keep you healthy, Aims."
"But I am healthy, Dad!"
"Yes, but they keep you from getting a serious disease."
She thought for a moment.
"Could I die? From a serious disease?"
"Well, yes, you could. You've seen children with bad illnesses."

She nodded.

"Well how come Christine died in the car? She got her shots."

"Aimee, there are no shots that can protect someone from dying in... a car crash, or..."

"Drown-ding?" she asked.

"Yes, children—and big people—can drown, but no shots can stop it from happening or save them."

"But Daddy, *how come Christine died?* She was just a little kid in first grade!"

(I can't wait till they start asking about where babies come from. It'll be much, much easier!)

"I know she was a little kid. Sometimes—but only sometimes—little kids die too. I'm just glad—real glad—that I still have you and Katie." And I hug her.

Whenever she asks those why? questions, I just hug her, try to answer them as best I can, and tell her how I miss their momma and Christine and grandparents too.

I made a meatloaf today. There is something comforting about being in a warm kitchen as sunlight streams through the windows, with bright snow all around outside. I was feeling good, almost joyous. The year is over. 1981 will be much better for me. How could it *possibly* be worse than 1980? (Maybe I shouldn't ask.) I was whistling, too, as I cooked up dinner. I almost stopped feeling happy—that sounds strange, doesn't it?—but I went right on being happy. I have paid dues. I *deserve* to be happy.

"Real potatoes! Daddy, remember when Mommy used to make us real potatoes?"

I looked wounded.

"I make us 'real potatoes', Aim."

"No you don't."

"But I make French fries you and Katie like—the skinny ones just like McDonald's."

She looked at me with a disapproving hand on her hips. If she had shaken her index finger the picture would've been perfect.

"Those," she haughtily informed me, "are not 'real.' Judy's mother made real ones in her oven."

"Ahhhh! You mean *baked* potatoes!"

"The ones with skin still on. *Real* potatoes. That's what I've been saying!"

My meatloaf came out like a rock. Hard as a boulder. Even Thelma and Snowball III/Crazy Boy won't eat it.

But the real potatoes were great.

ta·ta·ta

I hired Lisa to baby-sit for the girls. I needed to take a walk. It was pretty cold today—about five below—and tonight it's about ten or fifteen below. As I walked past the silent frozen pond and red grist mill across from the house, I saw incredibly brilliant stars. I stopped, overcome by the thought that Chrissie already knew the mystery of death! And I—a part of her— knew the mystery, too. I was sharing this incredible puzzle with her, for we had talked and thought over so much in the fourteen years we had known each other. We talked about love, life, death, children, sex, wealth, politics, poverty.

Sharing this mystery with her tells me there is no "thinking" or analyzing death and dying. Chrissie is not thinking any longer; that's what living people do. The experience of death transcends thought. I feel her in me, and I—right now—feel a little bit of the peace she is feeling. In a way, part of me is dead; has died. But that is not bad or sad. It just is. Death is to be felt, not thought.

Even Aimee in her five-year-old way has the same perception of puzzlement and it is mixed with sorrow. As she sat on the sofa watching *Sesame Street* with Katie, I walked by and noticed she was upset: sucking her thumb and holding her ragged, pink, satin-edged blanket. She looked at me with a tear in her eye.

"Momma said she'd never die."

I sat next to her. We hugged.

"Aims, I don't think Momma said 'never,' she just..."

"Daddy, she said she wouldn't die for a long, long, long, long time."

I put my arm around her. She tilted her head toward my chest and sucked her thumb furiously. There was pain in her eyes. After a long quiet, she looked up at me.

"Dad, I know you miss her too. After all, you were her boyfriend and her husband and you liked her too. Didn't you?"

I didn't stop crying that night, but it was half out of missing everyone, and half out of happiness and appreciation for still having my Katie and Aimee with me. And out of knowing the mystery of death.

ta·ta·ta

Happy New Year! I drank too much at the New Year's Eve party at Town Hall in Reading. Had a great time dancing and singing till I was hoarse.

Fuck 1980. It has been a schizoid, happy-then-horrible year. A hateful, painful year.

ta·ta·ta

Looked back on the past six months. What was the hardest thing about surviving—outliving—your spouse? Being "keeper of memories." Like most married couples and close friendships, there were things only we two shared, and now I'm left alone to preserve the memory of those events. For example, Aimee used to make strange, bird-like cooing noises as she sat in her crib... only Chrissie and I knew about them. Or how about the time little Christine took her first steps at nine months of age? She suddenly got up and ran along the sidewalk outside our Brooklyn apartment. Not one other living person remembers her red velveteen dress that day, her chubby thighs hustling back and forth, and the gratified expression on her face when she finally plopped down. Chrissie, you've left me with a "marriage of one." It is so dreary being sole curator of the "Bob and Chris Museum." It is hard, and very unsatisfying.

My dear sweetheart. I miss you; I love you, but please forgive me if I start putting away our exhibits.

July 20, 1970—Newlyweds walking out of church in Brooklyn.
Inset: At the reception we toast each other. *Credit: DiGiulio Collection*

We make our move to
Vermont.
Credit: DiGiulio Collection

Our first home is heated
solely by wood.
Credit: DiGiulio Collection

March 1978. Chrissie and I are expecting Katie. *Credit: DiGiulio Collection*

Our first complete family portrait, at the 1979 Vermont State Fair (l to r) Aimee, Chrissie, Christine, Katie, and "Ulysses S." DiGiulio. *Credit: DiGiulio Collection*

Three sisters pose for their first "sisters dressed alike" portrait.
Inset: Christmas 1979: Katie, Aimee, and Christine visit Santa.
Credit: DiGiulio Collection

Mother-in-law, Olga, in Hawaii and father-in-law, Paul, shortly before their last visit with us in Vermont. *Credit: DiGiulio Collection*

Early in 1980, savoring
my new book!
Credit: DiGiulio Collection

Burial was on Sunday. *Credit: DiGiulio Collection*

Aimee wanted us to get the heart-shaped headstone. We did. *Credit: DiGiulio Collection*

Just like family.
Friends Neil and
Anne Marinello,
with Kyle, Heather,
and Brent.
Credit:
DiGiulio Collection

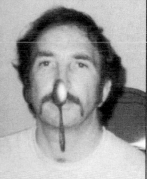

Back home finally. My friend Paul
Robbins lightens the mood.
Credit: DiGiulio Collection

We couldn't have made it without my sister and her family: Ann and Frank
Vega with Frankie and Angela Rose... nor without Chrissie's sister Paula Leskiw
(with Katie). *Credit: DiGiulio Collection*

Swimming at Stoughton Pond. *Credit: DiGiulio Collection*

Katie, Dad, and Aimee celebrate Dad's new hairdo. *Credit: DiGiulio Collection*

Early 1983. My "girlfriend" Emily and I at Hardee's after classes. *Credit: DiGiulio Collection*

I propose marriage to Emily in December 1983. *Credit: DiGiulio Collection*

May 1984. I receive my doctor of philosophy degree from the University of Connecticut. Emily received her masters there earlier. *Inset:* My brother Tommy celebrates our graduation. *Credit: DiGiulio Collection*

Our wedding. The temperature climbed to 100º F. *Credit: DiGiulio Collection*

June, 1984. Wedding in New Jersey. (l to r) Mom's friend Tom, Mom, Emily, Bob, my sister, Ann, and brother, Tommy. Attendants Katie and Aimee.
Credit: DiGiulio Collection

Christmas 1984, in Connecticut.
Credit: DiGiulio Collection

August 14, 1986: Running in
election for probate judge.
Credit: DiGiulio Collection

Robert C. DiGiulio Seeks Probate Judge Position

Taftsville resident Robert C. DiGiulio has announced his candidacy for Probate Judge of Hartford District in Windsor County.

ROBERT C. DiGIULIO

Presently working as an educational consultant, Dr. DiGiulio has written for numerous magazines and newspapers on the subject of family, and has authored two books, *When You Are A Single Parent*, and *Effective Parenting*. The latter has now been released in Spanish translation.

Formerly a widower, and having been through the process of probate in Vermont, DiGiulio has expressed a strong belief that the Probate Judge should be not only capable, but compassionate as well. "People pass through the Probate process at difficult times in their lives — whether they're widowed or they're young children in need of a guardian, the Probate Judge must be someone responsive not only to the letter of the law, but aware of the disruption of the family which is taking place."

Dr. DiGiulio has served as principal at Bridgewater and Windsor elementary schools, and has taught at Pomfret and Reading. He has lectured extensively on the subjects of widowhood and single parenting, and in 1985 he guided the establishment of a self-help group for the widowed in Windsor County. DiGiulio is now remarried and resides in Taftsville with his wife and three children.

Dr. DiGiulio, the only non-attorney in the Democratic slate, has two masters degrees, and recently earned his Doctor of Philosophy Degree in Family Relations from the University of Connecticut in May 1984, which included studying Family Law at the University of Connecticut's School of Law. He is a member of the American Psychological Association, and the National Council on Family Relations.

DiGiulio is one of four Democrats seeking their party's nomination for the Probate Judge post. Others are William Donahue of Hartland, David Herlihy of South Royalton, and Judith Miller Kasper of Norwich.

The lone Republican candidate for the post is Bonnie Adams Umland of Woodstock.

Aimee and Katie hold new
sister, Angela.
Credit: DiGiulio Collection

October 1986. Back to Florida as a new family. *Credit: DiGiulio Collection*

December 1988. Our new family is complete: proud sisters with new baby brother, Matthew. *Credit: DiGiulio Collection*

Matthew and
Angela today.
Credit:
DiGiulio Collection

Aimee and Katie
today. *Credit:*
DiGiulio Collection

Em and I today. *Credit: DiGiulio Collection*

PART THREE: LATER ON

One cannot live with the dead;
either we die with them,
or we make them live again.
Or we forget them.
                    —Louis Martin-Chauffier

I can tell I'm moving on to a new "stage": I still think about Chrissie each day, but (I confess) hours now pass when I do not dwell on her. I feel guilty as I type this out right now. As if I'm betraying her memory. I find that (I have written the word "I" nine times so far!) I am thinking more and more about what I've got to do with my life. For example, this morning after I made a tasty omelet for the girls' breakfast ("Flat eggs again?"), they went to play in the other room. And it sounds corny but it was the first time I was alone yet felt glad that I was alive. Alive for my kids, alive for myself. I mean, I could be dead myself just as easily, perhaps, as my wife passed through the world. I am not one bit more invulnerable than she was. Chrissie's death has made me very aware of how slight the thread is that holds us to life.

I am also happy to be alive for her. My survival is her survival as well. If she isn't here, I am here for her.

Yes, I am in the third stage—my "advanced stage" of grief— I am emerging, reawakening, coming in, coming out, and coming to. I am crawling out of a very dark and very scary cave.

Katie needs socks. I need ice cream. Stopped for ice cream, then went to Kmart. I carried Katie into the store. I usually do this—carry her—upon entering and exiting Kmart-type stores. This way we quickly buzz past the machines filled with candy and gumballs, and plastic balls of slimy goo, and most especially those huge "whopper" gumballs the size of a golf ball upon

which a child can gag and suffocate—how can they legally sell
gumballs that big? Besides, with the remains of her drippy
cone, there's no place to fit more goodies.

And as usual I was the only man among women in the
toddler's section, all of them rooting through Sesame Street
underwear, Strawberry Shortcake dresses, and teensy blouses
and booties. It all looks like dolls' clothing to me.

Did you know that kids' socks have sizes? What is her size
in socks? They all look so small! Cannot even remember her
shoe size. I must have appeared puzzled or helpless, for an
immense woman—with arms like Popeye—leaned toward me.
She smelled of cigarettes and was panting.

"Look on the back. Find her shoe size," she pointed, took a
breath and continued, "and there's where her socks size is."

I thanked her. We exchanged other small talk, and I went
to the cashier. As I dug for my wallet I sat Katie on the counter.
She sucked at the gummy remains of a chocolate cone that
suddenly slid down her chin onto her blouse.

"Ohh! Mommy's going to be mad at you!" the cashier said.

Katie mumbled back at her.

Looking at me over her eyeglasses the cashier added, "And
she should be mad at you too!"

Trying to stop her from continuing the "Mommy" chatter
and having Katie either feel bad or spill the beans, I kind of
leaned over to catch her ear and murmured,

"Well, uh, actually, you see, I, uh, lost my wife, and..."

Without missing a beat, the cashier gazed past my shoulder
and vigorously shook her head.

"She's right there—isn't that her?" innocently pointing to
the massive, panting woman now looking at handbags.

"Oh," was all I could say. Yeah. My wife. Yeah! Aha! There
she's been all along! Thank you, thank you, thank you.

I walked out of Kmart with wet eyes. Tears of laughter. As I
waited for dear, Huge Henrietta, my precious wife.

❧❧❧

Took the girls to the hair salon in Windsor. They look
absolutely gorgeous! Aimee charmed the hairdressers and
customers by telling them that, when she was done, she was
going to go to the doctor to get her shot for "chicken pops."
"What?" they giggled. "Chicken pops!" she repeated. And again.
"What?" they giggled. "Chicken 'P-O-P-S'."

But as we drove up to the house, I asked Aimee if she

wanted to hear a funny story; an old story that involved her Mom. Aimee said, "No" and left the room. It seems like whenever I bring up her mother's name, Aimee withdraws. It's better for me to just let her bring it up when she feels like talking.

ta.ta.ta.

Went to the Harry Chapin concert at Rutland High School, and I think it helped me to realize how important people are to me. I hear that Harry Chapin donates half of all he earns from his concerts to charity. Tonight Harry had his seven-year-old son Josh on stage with him; the boy did a little dance to one of his dad's tunes. There was an unmistakable gleam in Harry's eyes; a gleam that began not when the audience applauded, not when he realized how much money the concert would raise for the Sugar Maple Rehabilitation Center, but when his little boy stood aside him, swaying to the music. When Chapin's intense guitar strumming ceased, he seemed tranquil, in harmony with all of us. I wish I had snapped a photo of Josh and Harry, smiling, looking at each other. Father of the year: Harry Chapin.

ta.ta.ta

It's incredibly cold this January morning: almost twenty below. I love Vermont when it is like this. That reverential, hushed feeling when it is very cold, cold even for Vermont. Everything outside is perfectly still—even the plume of smoke rising from each chimney looks like an unmoving gray curtain. I wish you could see out my kitchen window. The dull red of the huge grist mill is the only color visible in a black and white picture. The pond is hidden under a dusting of snow, and the mill wheel is frozen, from rust as well as from frost. This morning makes the classic calendar picture of Vermont in winter. Footprints across the pond; an enormous blue jay is unmoving, caught in the act of raiding Aimee's bird feeder. Moments like this make me blissful because the largeness of nature overpowers feelings of gloom, anger, or fear. Beside nature, bereavement seems so puny.

Widowed people become frozen too; frozen in time. It really is like being an exhibit in a museum. Part of my job in "getting well" is to create new joys, not to recreate old ones. Get out of the museum, even as comfortable and safe as it feels. I have to get out. The joys I shared with my in-laws, who were fine and precious, cannot be shared anymore. The most intimate and personal joys I shared with Chrissie and Christine are memories now; I've got to start making new memories. And I want Katie and Aimee to grow up as well as they can, without their living in a past they hardly knew. A museum is educational for visitors, but is deadly for fools who try to inhabit it.

ᶻᵃᶻᵃᶻᵃ

I have to do it. Today. I am going to hire a baby-sitter and drive to Boston. By myself. I want to locate Custer's restaurant and see Liane. I have been thinking of her for too long now and am excited by the idea we might meet again.

10:00 a.m. I called Custer's. No answer. Yet it was early; most city restaurants don't open till mid-afternoon.

As I drove along the Massachusetts Turnpike, I found myself whistling, and singing along with the radio. I opened all the windows and blasted the radio as I helped Del Shannon sing "Runaway." My little runaway... A-run, run, run, run, runaway.

As Del Shannon faded from my head, Liane walked right in:

> You live in Vermont? Why Bob, I love the country... I was raised in the country, and yes, I'd be so happy to live there with you... We could open a natural food store—you grow the organic veggies, and I sell them! We could even someday get married and have children. Aimee and Katie would love to have a little sister or brother! Once a month, we'll drive into Boston for theater or to Montreal for opera, and if you'd like, we could take in a baseball game! (Lucky me! I had prayed she'd be a baseball fan!)

After parking in a huge, concrete, multi-level garage downtown, I bought a Boston street map. The garage was right near Quincy Market and Fanueil Hall—the only places I'd ever been to in Boston. As I walked (and walked) toward Custer's the neighborhood got pretty raw looking. I'd heard of Boston's "combat zone"—its red-light district. Could this be it? Eventually I found the block, but saw no restaurant. I checked the next block, but no luck. I asked a guy where Custer's was, and he pointed me right back to where I had stopped the first time.

Indeed, Custer's was there—I had walked past it. There was no marquee or advertising sign. Instead, a bleak storefront. "Custer's Last Stand" was a bar. Most of its front window was painted black on the inside. At eye level was an unpainted rectangle. I looked through at a pasteboard that announced tonight's show of "exotic dancers":

"YOU CAN'T HANDLE ONE. CAN YOU IMAGINE FOUR? CHERI likes them 'tall,' ASHLEY likes them 'sweet,' LIANE likes them 'rich,' and CINDY likes them... 'discreet'."

Cheri, Ashley, Liane, and Cindy.

Liane?

My organic vegetarian Liane?

I could have denied it was Liane if not for the black and white glossy publicity photo showing her standing chorus-line with three other women. They looked at once snazzy and sleazy, smiling and hard-faced, self-assured yet victimized. I was heartbroken.

Before I walked away I looked at Liane's clear eyes—I wished her well. It felt good to be able to say good-bye.

※※※

In today's *Sunday Boston Globe* there was an ad in the travel section for a Barbados cruise. "Jazz Me to Barbados" is what they called it. Intrigued, I phoned my sister Ann and told her and Frank about it. They thought it was a great idea. They offered (as usual) to mind Aimee and Katie if I decided to go. Hmmm, Barbados. The ad promised nonstop jazz and rock musicians playing all the way to the islands.

Ann said, "Why wait? If you don't go now, when will you get another chance?"

"But the money," I said.

Frank got on the phone. He said they'd give me money just to get rid of me. Besides, they'd love to have the girls stay.

I'll call tomorrow. With the temperature outside minus 1° F., Barbados sounds alluring.

※※※

Barbados is alluring. Temperature: 77° F. That's *plus* 77° F. I called the agency in Boston. They'll send me the brochures, trip planner, and literature about the cruise ship.

※※※

Spring is finally here. I tilled the garden last week with my trusty Troy Bilt rototiller. (You have to wait several days after tilling before planting, because the soil has to harden a bit. The first year I planted all my seeds right away and the seeds eventually slid down to Hades.) Lettuce and peas always go in first in spring, and today was the day. Katie helped me by meticulously placing each pea two inches apart and in a straight line in the little trench. She looked up and beamed. I praised her work.

"Great job, Kate!"

I had her spit out the pea she was chewing.

Aimee stood by, impatiently wanting to know why we were planting "dead peas." And when we began planting spinach seeds, Aimee left in a froth.

"Gross! I hate spinach, Dad! You and Katie can have it all for yourselves."

I also splurged and bought a dozen hyacinths to plant.

(Doesn't the word "splurged" sound offensive? "Doctor, my wife splurged this morning!" "Oh, dear. Where did it happen?" "In the living room... all over the carpet.")

The publishing rights to my book *Effective Parenting* have been sold to New Century Publishers in Piscataway, New Jersey.

Of all places.

Piscataway.

Like "splurged."

I splurged in Piscataway.

People think writers are rich. Ha! My hardcover parenting book has sold well, but would have done much better as a paperback. My little paperback *When You Are a Single Parent* has almost sold out of its first printing of ten thousand. Sounds impressive, until you realize I get only five percent of the cover price.

At $1.95 per book, I earn nine and three-fourths of a cent per book.

Math problem: If an author earns 9.75 cents per book, how much will he earn if ten thousand books are sold? Extra Credit: How long will it take for him to be forced to stop writing and start selling life insurance?

❧❧❧

How could I say nothing more about Barbados? Tonight I returned from my one-week "Jazz Me to Barbados" cruise!

Until I saw the ad for the cruise, I never even gave Barbados a thought. But my sister and brother-in-law's urging really did convince me, along with the idea of jazz and rock musicians playing through each night. And the nonstop parties! Single women! Food galore! And if I could only find at least one other guy to share a cabin, the rate would be within my budget. If I could get two or three guys to share a cabin, it would be even less. I called four friends, but each turned me down. Their reasons were, respectively: "I'm working and can't take the time off"; "I'm too poor"; "I get seasick looking at an aquarium"; and my last hope told me, "My wife said she'd break my legs."

Undaunted I called the friendly-sounding cruise agent in Boston. I explained to Marcy that I was single... no, not divorced, uh, widowed. (When will I learn to stop saying the "w" word?) Are there cheap cabins available? I couldn't afford a private accommodation. "Piece of cake," Marcy told me. "We arrange roommates all the time," and—lucky me—she'd just received a call from someone ("Spanish... is that okay?") who also wanted to share a cabin. Marcy told me she'd check and call me back.

I thought about sharing a cabin with a total stranger: After all, we'd share only the cabin. The rest of the time he'd go his way and I'd go mine. His being Spanish didn't matter at all. But I was leery of being stuck with a politician, a lawyer, or— worst of all—a life insurance salesman.

Within an hour, I heard from Marcy. She was exuberant.

"Bob, it's all set! Found the perfect roommate for you!"

Not *a roommate*, but *the perfect roommate*, she emphasized.

I began to feel excited. What luck!

"Great, Marcy! Can you tell me something about him?"

"Well, there's something I didn't tell you at first—I wanted to make sure before telling you. You are open-minded, aren't you, Bob?"

"I don't care that he's Spanish, or anything."

"Well, that's not the problem," she said.

Uh-oh. A neo-Nazi lawyer who sells life insurance and plays the accordion.

"I... guess so," I answered, thinking I should back out. (What? Selfishly go on a cruise? And take food out of my children's mouths?)

"Your roommate's name is Rita. She's a nurse—cardiac intensive care—at 'Mass General' Hospital, and this is sad, I know, but she's also a widow!"

A woman?

A widow?

I was stunned. Before I could talk, Marcy gave me Rita's number, and before I could think, I called her.

"'allo?" the voice asked. "Oo ees dees?"

In her broken English, Rita told me how her problem was the same as mine: She really wanted to go on this cruise, but couldn't find someone on short notice to share a cabin. Between her high-pressure job and the stress of losing her husband, she was exhausted, and her family insisted she go. How did she feel about sharing with a guy? It didn't bother her, and she would simply lie to her family, telling them about "Roberta," a sweet Italian roommate who shared a cabin with her.

A woman? She wants to share a cabin with me?

Sure.

Once on board the boat I found the cabin. I thought it was a mistake—a closet, not a room. Certainly not for two people. But two tiny beds were there, separated by a narrow aisle and a four-drawer dresser. There was even a minute bathroom and a small sofa under a porthole. I began unpacking, putting my things in the bottom two drawers of the dresser. Our dresser. I felt nervous; like a newlywed in one of those arranged marriages where you don't meet until after the ceremony.

A knock on the door.

"Rita?"

She nodded and shook my hand.

"Hi, roommate!" she said, pushing in her bag-on-wheels with her foot. With brilliant black eyes and long black hair, she looked to be in her mid-forties.

"Just call me Roberta!" I said, and we laughed.

The first night out we went to dinner together—"escorts" to each other. Getting dressed for dinner was odd; comfortable having Rita there to talk to, and to take turns as clothes critic and fashion consultant. After dinner, we went our separate ways. At night, I got in at around 2:00 a.m. Undressing by the stream of moonlight coming through the porthole, I said good night to the lump of blankets I imagined to be Rita, but she was long gone.

The next night, as we lay in our beds in total darkness, we talked. Her husband Jorge had been professor of economics at either Boston College or a Boston college (I can't remember) and like Chris and me, they had been married just shy of ten years. Shortly after they planned to return to the Princess resort in Barbados for their second honeymoon, Jorge died suddenly of a heart attack. Now Rita was returning, on her own.

She and Jorge had been expert dancers; she taught me how to do a cha-cha in the narrow space between our beds. But the best memories I have are of gossiping about the weird people on the cruise, "comparing notes," and analyzing the mating habits of the passengers. On our boat, relationships started quickly and ended quickly. Like clothes shoppers on a spree that would end at midnight, singles tried each other on in rapid succession. Perhaps it was due to the urgency to meet "Mr. or Ms. Right," and thus have one's investment in the cruise pay off.

Rita and I met each evening for dinner ("our date" she called it), but otherwise were on our own, occasionally meeting at the ship's disco and sharing a drink or dance. We got to do our cha-cha to live music. She was great; her feet didn't seem to touch the floor. I stunk, almost knocking over a waitress. But we were laughing so much it didn't matter. As we danced the slow dances, people whom we had joked about the night before in our cabin would glide by, and Rita would only have to look at me for us both to be in stitches.

And of course, there was a price to pay. Word got around. We were an item. Least enthralled with our arrangement were the proper Dutch hosts running the cruise. Toward the end of each cruise, a special dinner is planned where the captain meets and greets each guest. As Rita and I greeted the captain and walked past the reception line, an official-looking guy in a white uniform motioned me aside.

"You are the one?"

"What 'one'?" I asked.

"Occupying cabin twelve on the Lido Deck?"

He was polite, reserved. I nodded.

"The one sharing a cabin with a woman?"

I nodded again. He stood stiffly.

"I am sorry, but it is a violation of Imperial-Dutch Lines policy" he explained, "to have mixed company stay in a cabin."

"Que pasa 'mixed company'?" (I hoped I got the Spanish right, but Rita's disdainful look told me, not even close.)

He shifted around nervously, "Uh, when adults
 who are not married stay together in the same cabin."

"Not married?" I asked, turning to Rita, who took on my equally-indignant expression.

"Who said we were not married?" I asked.

I held out my left hand to him. He saw my wedding band.

Rita echoed, "Yes, who?" (She looked savage. Even scared me.)

His white face turned scarlet.

Rita extended her left hand. (Not only did she have a wedding band, but a huge rock that looked like two carats. Jorge must've done well, practicing what he preached in his economics classes.)

He looked stricken. He mumbled an apology.

"So good to meet you!" she purred as she took his hand.

Rita turned to me, "Come on, Honey, we eat now."

He walked away shaking his head.

Later that night, Rita and I would re-enact the scene three times for friends at our nightclub table. We changed it each time to exaggerate his indignant expression. "Capitan Harumph" we called him.

I enjoyed sightseeing in Barbados, but other than my time with Rita, did not enjoy the social life and the analytical, intense scrutiny: Who are you, what do you do, how much do you make, are you gay, are you cheating on your wife, et cetera. But most of all, I learned that revealing that you're a *widowed person* can be a bummer, and unless you are a *wealthy* (elderly) *widowed person*, that revelation will immediately snuff out any possibility of romantic furtherances.

She: "Do you live in Noo Yawk, too?"

Me: "No, I live in Vermont. But I was born and raised in New Y...."

She: (foggily) "Vermont? Where is that in? Is it upstate Noo Yawk?"

Me: (amiably) "No, but it's near. By the way, my name's Bob DiGiulio."

She: (recognition) "Oh, you're the writer sharing a cabin with a woman, right?"

Me: (uncertainly) "Yeah. But we're really not..."

She: (emotes) "Outrageous! I think that's real super."

Me: "Well, uh... I didn't get your name..."

She: "Oh, sorry. My name's Pam (or Nan or Fran)."

Me: "May I buy you a..."

She: "A Tab will be fine."

Me: (to bartender) "Two Tabs, please!"

She: (making eye contact for first time) "Isn't this a neat cruise?"

Me: "Having a fine time! Glad I came!"

She: (stirring her Tab) "Are you solo? I mean, except for your roommate?"

Me: "... am I really married?"

She: (laughs) "Yea, I guess that's what I mean!"

Me: (shakes head) "No, I'm not. You know, I am surprised how many guys on this boat are married, but are pre..."

She: "Divorced?"

Me: (adrenaline starts) "No, I'm a... I'm, uh,..."

She: (giggles) "Don't tell me: A virgin!"

We: (hearty laughter) (Did you ever find your toes curling, saying in rhythm, oy **vey**, oy vey, oy vey? That's what mine were doing.)

Me: "Actually, I'm widowed. My wife..."

She: (somber, eyes lowered) "Oh! I'm sorry. I am so sorry to hear that."

She drank the rest of the Tab and left.

Being thirty-two and widowed is a show-stopper.

As we packed our bags and were ready to "deship" (the captain's actual word), I hugged Rita.

I said, "I'll miss you!"

She said, "Of course! But we must promise each other to be happy from now on, and think of all the funny things we did if we get sad."

She held out her finger with her wedding band: "And don't you dare forget our anniversary, sweetie!"

ⓉⓉⓉ

I have thought about the cruise each day, and what a great time I had. I needed it. It was a perfect time-out from my pain; from missing everyone so much.

As June wears on, my mood is being brought lower and lower. The very idea of the month—June—brings me back a year. I feel like I'm backsliding a little. Not depressed like before, but down.

ⓉⓉⓉ

Today's Friday, June 26, 1981. It's been exactly one year. A year ago today. A scorching-hot Thursday when I went to play tennis. I remember Chrissie not wanting to kiss me (draaaa-gon mouth!). I hear a voice that is my daughter Christine calling "Maaaaaa!" from inside the house. I wave to Chrissie and drive away and never see her again. Just like that. It ended just like that.

But wait! Maybe not. As I drive away, I look in my rearview mirror—she's turning in the doorway and going back inside. I look through the windshield, but... Hey, stupid, look in the side-view mirror! You forgot to bring in the newspaper, Bobo, and that's your job. I smack my forehead, turn the Rabbit around and drive back up the driveway. Get out. Get the newspaper. No, not on the passenger's seat—bring it inside, Blockhead. There's Chrissie, making breakfast for Christine, Aimee, and Katie. Her dad and mom are still asleep—they love hot weather. I put the newspaper on the table. I hold my wife in my arms. "Please stay home today," I ask her. "Please don't go."
Please.
Don't go.

This year has been an eternity—the longest year of my life. It feels like a lifetime has passed for me, but it's only been a year. I am much older than I was a year ago. Today wasn't as bad as I had worried it would be. People do strange things on the anniversary of unhappy events in their lives.
I'm tired, very tired of this grief stuff. I'm impatient. I want to get on with the "new me."

I want Aimee and Katie to grow past their pain, too. When I bring up Chrissie's name, it seems to make them sad. Their voices become serious, their eyes fall a bit. They play and laugh and tease like normal children, yet... I worry. They don't want to talk about IT any more.

I went to the cemetery today; only the fourth time I've gone since the burial. It always seemed a little senseless to me that people intentionally go to a cemetery, only to be miserable there and cry a lot. I went, and felt miserable there and cried a lot.
But cemeteries do make sense: By using the cemetery as a sort of barometer, people can "measure" their pain and judge how they now feel compared to previous visits. A cemetery is a constant, is unchanging. By placing myself in the backdrop of a timeless cemetery, I see change in myself. Like my father's 1953 Buick that, to a boy, seemed the size of a battleship.
And once I entered the cemetery and felt pangs of sadness, I knew right away that my pain is less than six months ago.

I've begun to understand that they have died (I can even speak the word now without a lump in my throat), and my new life is starting to take shape. Although I wasn't aware of it at the time, from the moment they died, I began to make over my life.

Yet it is a tug-of-war: letting go, then pulling back. Pulling back and pulling back more, then letting go. Needing to let go then wanting to let go, then not wanting to let go. I was lucky. I fought letting go furiously at first, but less and less as the year went on. Some people fight it—successfully—for the rest of their lives.

I *am* better. I *can* read books and newspapers now. The dull headache *has* gone. I *can* get interested in which variety of peas to plant in my garden. I *don't* feel guilty anymore if I haven't thought of them until two or three hours have passed in the morning. I have fundamentally changed, although I still miss them terribly and usually cry at night for them. A tug-of-war.

Crying helps. I used to think it was a waste of time. Not because it was un-manly to cry, but because it was, well, dumb. Non-productive. But I have learned how wrong I was. Crying is as important to a person in pain as a lifeboat is to a non-swimmer flailing in the sea. Every night when I am alone I sit on her side of the bed and I cry. And after, I do feel better. In fact, I cry at night while watching TV, and even while I play my new Atari video game. Pow... pow... pow... I wonder what I must look like crying as I shoot down the aliens in "Space Invaders."

Allow yourself to cry. No, I'll go one better: Become an *active crier*. Plan to set aside time for crying: Pick a time and a place. And cry. Cry royally and lustfully. It helps sleep, appetite, mood, everything.

ᴈᴀᴈᴀᴈᴀ

Rita sent me a letter. She enclosed a picture of her two sons. She missed our good jokes and company. I wrote back and invited her to visit me, take in some of the tourist traps in Vermont. Outlet stores. Maple syrup. Cheeses.

The more I think about my future, the more I am sure that I really want to go back to college and work toward my doctoral degree. This evening, I received the last of the three college catalogs I had requested from Cornell, University of Connecticut, and Harvard. They each have doctoral programs in "human development."

Me, at Harvard?

As I looked over the catalogs over dinner, I could tell that Harvard's program was not really what I wanted. The University of Connecticut and Cornell programs look ideal. They'd permit me more flexibility in designing my doctoral studies plan. I guess being allowed to attend Harvard is enough of a reward. Like dining at the finest of restaurants, you gratefully take what artistry the chef deigns to prepare.

≥a≥a≥a

We are now into the second year... after That Day. I still miss Chrissie, but the pain is less. No longer an ache or a hurt; it's more like missing someone. My daughter Christine is another matter. I feel confused about her. I'm her father and I failed. At the most primitive, male level, I feel failure: I failed to keep my daughter safe and protect her from death. I cried for a half-hour today for Christine. She has been in the shadow of my pain for Chrissie over this past year, yet since she was born, Christine had a special place in my heart and always will. My little girl, I miss you so much and will never understand. How? Why?

≥a≥a≥a

Labor Day is gone and today Aimee and Katie are back in school. Katie's in the preschool program and Aimee starts first grade! They have matching dresses—Strawberry Shortcake. Sent by Grandma. I wouldn't stoop to buying them those outfits. I took pictures of them on the first day and brought them both to school. I can always use those snapshots for blackmail when they are teenagers.

I came home to do the laundry. As the washer filled, I emptied Aimee's pockets. In her jeans pocket was the most grotesque-smelling and looking object I ever saw. It looked like a mouse had crawled into her pocket, died there, and begun to rot.

Holding my nose, I held the pocket over the garbage and shook it out, then threw the pants into the washer.

She had worn the jeans only a couple of days earlier—she spent most of that day with her friend Hillary. What the hell could that thing be?

But there are larger questions in my life, and I still seek answers to them. Even though I've come quite far, I want answers. I look back at my book *When You Are a Single Parent,* and I feel somewhat reassured. I will never forget the first time I ventured into the Dartmouth Bookstore (the greatest bookstore in the world) about a year ago. Guided by remote control (Answers! Get the book with the answers!), I went to the section with books about death. But when I got there I was repelled by some; they seemed flowery, gratuitous, and far-too-fragrant works of poetry that I could not relate to—there could be no answers there. At the "child care" counter, I picked up a voluminous manual for single fathers (me? a "single father"?) and flipped through the index, locating, "Death, telling children about." Upon finding the page, I swear this is what it said: "Death is an especially difficult subject for children to understand." Period. That was it, besides two additional sentences about "understanding" and "communication." Apparently, death was an especially difficult subject for the author to understand (and communicate) as well.

I glanced around the store—a man was looking through fiction paperbacks; an old lady was in the next aisle near the gardening books; a group of teenage girls were examining books on craft and pottery, and here I was—the only one reading the stupid books on death. I remember feeling very lonely, then angry for it. I imagined walking up to each of the happy browsers and asking them point-blank: "Don't you realize that someday you too will lose somebody you love?" How could I be the only one rummaging through bereavement books? Death is a reality for everyone. "Stop denying reality," I almost shouted. "Come on over here now and pick out a book! It's never too soon!" If I did shout that, however, I'd spend time not in the Dartmouth Bookstore but in the Dartmouth Medical Center. But you know, it's true: We really do have to make believe death doesn't await us in order to go about our business. If we spent our days pondering our death, we would become paralyzed.

After thinking this, I remember leaving the bookstore, getting in my car, and crying as I drove all the way home. I felt better.

When I got home I saw her now clean pants in the dryer. I asked her what it was that was in her pocket. She thought for a moment.

"Oh, yeah Dad. You know when I ate over at Hillary's house?"

Yes, I remembered.

"Well, her Mom made this really strange dinner. I think they bought cheap meat. It was so hard I couldn't chew it or eat it or nothing, so every time I put a piece in my mouth, I tried chewing it. Then I made believe I had a cough, and I coughed it into my hand. And I coughed every time I had a piece. And then I just pushed the pieces in my pocket. I didn't want to hurt their feelings, Dad. I think they don't have enough money to buy good food like hamburgers and hot dogs like we do."

❧❧❧

Great news: I have been accepted into the doctoral program at the University of Connecticut. I could start as soon as January.

I went to a retreat weekend in Rhode Island held by THEOS. It's a national support network for widowed people that stands for "They Help Each Other Spiritually." Founded by Mrs. Bea Decker in the early 1960s, THEOS has grown quickly, with chapters in many states and several Canadian provinces.

These workshops are very helpful for my spiritual side. Since I do not attend regular religious services, I feel a little bit like an outsider in spiritual matters.

At one of the workshops, the leader was a widowed woman who put the pain of being widowed into an interesting perspective. She said that the important thing about bereavement is not the gaping wounds that we all felt, but the healing scar tissue. "Martyrs with wounds still fresh will have to wait... to get into heaven, wounds have to be scars. Anyone can bleed, but it takes courage to allow your wounds to form scar tissue and heal," she said.

❧❧❧

The big move. It's all set. After Christmas, I'm taking Katie and Aimee and we're all going to Connecticut. To live for a while with Aunt Ann and Uncle Frank. And Grandma DiGiulio, whose home is five minutes away from them. Ann and Frank are excited that we're coming, and Katie and Aimee are looking forward to it, too.

It means I will withdraw Aimee from the Reading School, and send her to Thomas J. Hooker School in Meriden. I already spoke with the school principal there, and met Aimee's teacher—an intelligent, creative woman. Katie has been enrolled in St. John's Lutheran Preschool along with her cousin, Frankie. The two of them get along well; almost like siblings. As for me,

I'll be going to the University of Connecticut, and have reserved a small dorm room in the graduate dormitory for the nights I stay late at the university.

ea·ea·ea

Here I am. Writing this in my dormitory room at the University of Connecticut. The girls are in school in Meriden, loving their visit with Aunt Ann and Uncle Frank. I have classes Monday through Thursday, then stay with everyone in Meriden Friday through Sunday.

What is it like here at the university? For someone who is an adult and has lived on his own, It is quite unreal.

Classes are absorbing, the faculty is articulate and scholarly, the library is outrageously well-stocked, but the social life here is dreadful. I am struck by how *serious* the students here appear to be. In or out of class, there's an absence of laughter; an atmosphere devoid of levity, silliness, or emotion. On the bathroom wall in the spotless, high-tech men's dorm was but one bit of graffito: Someone wrote "Ye must be born again." Under which was written, "Oh, my poor mother!"

Maybe I'm sour because of last night when I went for my first dip in the Alumni Hall pool. Splendid pool! Someone raised on the beach at Coney Island appreciates an inviting pool as few can. But as soon as I jumped in, I was waved ashore by a slender lifeguard.

"You can't do that," she yelled. Hard to hear her.

"Why not?" I asked, then realized I didn't know what I wasn't supposed to do.

She stared at me, petulant. I sucked in my gut. Maybe she likes me.

"You have to swim in the lanes!" she yelled back, pointing at the water.

A girl/woman with goggles stopped to help clarify.

"Like... you're not supposed to swim backwards?"

"Backwards? I don't even know *how* to..."

"No, like you're supposed to swim in the same direction as, like, everybody else?" (All her sentences ended in question marks. Perhaps she was Yiddish?)

I understood. Okay, like, I understand. Like the black lines at, like, the bottom of the pool. Like I'm supposed to follow them and swim like in line like part of a school of fish. Like where did you learn to speak? Like I'm leaving if I can't just slosh around. Jeez! Can't a guy just have fun?

"And cut-offs aren't allowed in the pool," the lifeguard added as I clomped off. I felt like peeing in her pool. Instead, I let out my gut.

I'm thirty-three, and everyone else in the university is about twenty or so. With my beard I must look like Father Time to these students. In the old days (1960s and 1970s) the older folks were the more serious students. Now it's reversed: The university may as well be a corporate boardroom of Lloyds of London, the joylessness is so rampant. Even a day-care center on campus is called the "Child Laboratory." God, how different all this is from the sixties. No *joie de vivre*.

The students seem educationally pre-programmed, like androids. The girls/women talk about tofu, herpes, and running. The boys/men in the locker room have hair dryers, talk to each other politely and in terms of how far they ran today or how many laps they did around the pool, and have neither acne nor anger. Everyone is immaculately clean. No one complains about girlfriends, about women, about sex. Nobody is married, and nobody talks about getting engaged. Nobody screams about politics or a scumbag professor or the cost of tuition or the need for student representation on the university senate. Nothing. Just running and "partying" (drinking beer) on Thursday nights.

But best of all was this: In the huge Student Union building—which looks about as warm as Chase Manhattan Bank headquarters in lower Manhattan—an activity room was packed last night with students watching *Blazing Saddles*. I stood in back of the packed house, entranced by Mel Brooks' classic campfire scene when, one-by-one, the cowboys "react" to the beans they've eaten. I laughed aloud. No one else laughed. Like stereotypical librarians with their hair in buns, four or five students immediately turned to me and, as if on cue, they said in unison:

"Shhhh-h-h!"

I got a letter from Rita. She asked me to write back and give my advice: She has met a man and they want to get married. (From the picture she sent, he looks like an elderly Charles DeGaulle.) However, her older son is not too pleased by the idea of having a stepfather. Poor baby. I told Rita about my college career, about Aimee and Katie, and my life. At the end my advice was that if she felt happy with her fiancé and looked forward to being with him, she should marry him. Especially if he knew how to cha-cha.

ꝫ₊ꝫ₊ꝫ₊

Tonight I found myself sitting at Hardee's in Storrs, Connecticut, with this gentle person named Emily, whom I met at the first meeting of our graduate class, "Parent Education."

"I know you're a musician," I told her as we awaited our order. There was something harmonious about her. Her eyes?

"Wait," I asked. "Let me guess: you play oboe. No. Clarinet...?"

Emily smiled. "Close! But no, actually, I'm a flutist."

"No kidding. What type of music do you play?"

"Oh, just about anything. Classical, popular pieces."

I told her how I played piano; I played the same type of pieces she played on the flute. Then we got to talking about college, about what had brought us to the University. Emily was here to study teacher education. I wanted to study widowhood.

"Widowhood," she repeated.

"Yeah."

I told her how I had been visiting support groups for widowed persons throughout the Northeast and Canada, and how I was studying the ways people recover from widowhood.

Because I felt so comfortable with her, I told Emily about the accident, how Chris and Christine had been killed in a crash near our home. She listened, and talked with me until Hardee's closed at 11:00. We switched booths every few hours. And I went home and cried, not out of missing Chrissie or out of guilt, but because I felt so comfortable and happy being with this person Emily that I could not believe my good fortune.

ꝫ₊ꝫ₊ꝫ₊

There is only one word that applies to how I feel when I'm with Emily: "happy." I feel *happy* when I am with her.

When I think of happiness, I think of the preaching of Dr. Wayne Dyer. Wayne was my professor for two of my counselor education courses at St. John's University, just before his best selling *Your Erroneous Zones* was published. In 1972 and 1973, Dyer seemed to take his manuscript with him everywhere— including to the bathroom, we students thought—and we teased him in class. For instance, we were unanimous about his book's proposed title: "'Erroneous zones' is a bad title, Wayne." A sorry play on the words "erogenous zones." Only professors, we said, would make the connection between "erogenous" and "erroneous." An "egregious" error, someone thought...

And I remember a couple of students wailing, "Wayne, not another self-help book; the market is already overcrowded!" We tried to ruffle his feathers, especially because he was so certain, so convinced his manuscript would be a best-seller.

But his timing was perfect. Today's newspaper listed the best selling books of the 1970s: Wayne Dyer's "not-another-self-help-book" was number one; *Your Erroneous Zones* was the best-selling nonfiction paperback of that decade. At first it was a flop in hard cover, I learned, and after being rejected by several paperback publishers, Dyer footed the bill for a paperback printing, filled his station wagon with hundreds of copies, and then literally drove around the United States pitching his book.

I remember Wayne as an intense and dynamic lecturer, but not a particularly cheerful person. In class, he spoke wistfully of his daughter, his recent divorce, and his feelings of having been abandoned as a child. Loss affects even number-one-selling authors. "But happiness is the way," he'd say, urging us to take charge of our lives. "You can't 'look for' happiness."

✥✥✥

Today's June 15 and I'm back home in Vermont. It's been almost three years. I hold a drinking cup in my hand. Did Chrissie ever see it? A book is on the table. Was it around when she was alive? A can of baking powder in the cabinet—yes, that had to be there, soy sauce in the refrigerator... as the three years passed, I both cut the ties to my past and yet clung desperately to them. Curator of the "Museum of Bob and Chris." What to save? What to toss out? What to give away? Should I save it just because it was around "then"? Should I save Chrissie's broken umbrella or any of a thousand other things? How about for the girls—as mementos? What is right?

Answers? They are there, but I must look within. Within myself and within a new "mini-family." Not the bitter fragment of a family I now head, but the little family that has a future and a tomorrow.

Now that three years have passed, I see that I am basically a new person. I am not the same. I mean literally, I am different. Only my name is the same. I feel as if I have been changed irrevocably, transformed into that person I now am.

Alan Paton, author of *Cry the Beloved Country* wrote about his feelings after his wife died. It describes my feelings perfectly:

Once before I wrote that my grief was done,
and then it suddenly returned...
But now it will not return again.
Something within me is waking from a long
sleep, and I want to live and move again.
Some zest is returning to me, some
immense gratefulness for those who love me,
some strong wish to love them also.
I am full of thanks for life. I have not
told myself to be thankful, I just am so...

In many ways, I am now different; like Paton, I have emerged from a deep, three-year-long sleep. That sleep has changed me irrevocably: my new persona combines both "zest" and "gratefulness." And I like this "new me" again, even if who I am is totally different from the "me" I spent thirty years working on.

Do I mourn the person I was? Not any longer. What has helped me overcome that mourning is that, like Paton, I have replaced my tears with my appreciation for those who show love to me, and with my desire to show them love as well.

This includes my children. Katie and Aimee have responded well to the caring they've received. They seem to value human relationships more than other kids their ages do. They are not morbid and they are often silly. And like all kids, their behavior can be annoying at times. But there's an unwritten code of protection among us. They've become "pro-Dad." I've awakened to find breakfast already made for me, complete with a daisy in a drinking glass (so what's wrong with a bitten hunk of salami, a granola bar, and Hawaiian Punch for breakfast?). They want me to be happy, and I treasure them for their caring and love.

Throughout my personal rage and grief, I know Aimee and Katie must be allowed to be children—I refuse to talk to them as if they're adults. Kids feel powerless enough. They need me not as a pal but as a parent. I cannot change what happened no matter what I do, but I refuse to compensate, to knock myself out by being either too lenient with them (to "make it up to them") or too strict, delivering the "now-that-Momma's-not-here" lectures. They're not grown-ups; they'll never replace Chrissie, and need never try to do so.

No more shrines, either. Just like millions of other widowed men and women, I hid away—in a top drawer of my/our dresser—a whole stash of "relics": Chrissie's perfume, her leftover deodorant, earrings, even the blouse she wore "the day before." But now, no more. I took Chrissie's perfumes, bath oil, and bottle of cologne, filled the tub for the girls, dumped in the sacred lotions, and let them have "a smelly bath." They loved it, and now I have room in my drawer for other things.

Along with them, I matter, too. In the middle of reading them a story one night in July, Aimee looked up at me and said, "Dad, I don't want a different Mom. Are you ever going to get married again?"

I smiled (mostly because it was one of those questions totally out of the blue. What does that have to do with Dr. Seuss's *Cat in the Hat*?), and said, "Maybe. I'm not sure. But if I do, it'll be someone very, very nice."

A little reassurance works wonders. She had to know that first, I have a life to live not only as a Dad but as a grown-up. Second, and just as important, she needed to trust me; the last thing I want to inflict upon them is a "wicked stepmother." Any woman I married would be special. And kind. And someone who was capable of loving me and the girls. And vice-versa.

What they need—more than all the "answers" in the world— is for me to be there, to give them a bath, to cut the last fudge brownie exactly down the middle, to remind them to feed the cats, to yell, "Get these dirty socks out from under the bed," and to give them firmness when needed and hugs always. If Chrissie were alive today, there's little more she would want for us, I know.

I came up with a great idea that might reduce the number of speeders on the highways. (Yes, I know. I am a broken record already on this subject.) It goes like this: I call it an "R.M.T.," which stands for "radar-mimicking transmitter." Installed in any automobile, truck or bus, it's a device that would emit a radar-type signal forward, backward, and perhaps in all directions. The purpose of that signal is to confuse and confound radar detectors, rendering them useless. This prevents speeding drivers who use radar detectors from having the chance to momentarily slow down. (You think guns are a problem in the U.S.A.? Remember that for each person killed by a gun or rifle, thirty-one die as a result of a motor vehicle "accident.")

❧❧❧

Whew, Christine, my little 'Tine. I take back, just a little, what I have written about my daughter, Christine. I can't go through the rest of my life unaccepting of losing her as a six-year-old. Maybe by sharing the love I would have shared with Christine with my two girls Aimee and Katie will help me "process" my missing her so much. After all, I do love my Aimee and Katie just as much as Christine, and with her death, maybe I can try to love them even more.

ﷺﷺﷺ

Our annual pilgrimage to Florida. Katie, Aimee, and I took Amtrak to sunny Florida. As a "bon voyage" gift for our trip, Emily baked a sack of chocolate chip and nut cookies. We stayed at Cocoa Beach and visited some close friends. We took in Disney World, World of Shopping, Sea World, Circus World. (I was expecting a World World.)

We saw the Magic Kingdom in one full day, mostly by timing our visits to different attractions perfectly. Katie LOVED the ride where they played "It's a Small World" and Aimee enjoyed seeing Cinderella's castle. And the parade! At the end of the day, I bought Aimee a small stuffed Mickey Mouse doll. Wow. Twelve bucks. Katie fell for a Pinocchio doll. But as we walked to the register, her eyes got large.

Uh-oh. On the shelf above the register, Katie saw a HUGE Pinocchio—about two feet tall. "I like that one, Dad." I quivered as the girl brought it down. Ouch—thirty-two bucks!

Crisis. What to do? As the girl waited at the register for my decision, I said, "Oh, okay, it is our vacation." I thought. "It is well-made," I said. (Now really—was I expert in judging the quality of a stuffed toy?) "And you really don't ask for too much anyway, Kate." Katie was in heaven. It was almost as tall as she was.

As I signed my traveler's checks, the cashier said, "So many parents go through the same problem. I think they purposely place the big stuffed toys up here just so kids can beg for a bigger one just before leaving!"

Sea World was enchanting; the girls especially liked a mime at the start of the Shamu show. As customers headed to find seats for the performance, the mime imitated them behind their backs—the already-seated crowd roared with laughter as he pushed out his tummy and waddled behind heavy people, swaggered behind tall guys with cowboy hats, and shook his hips as he followed attractive women to their seats.

After saying goodbye to our friends, we headed for Circus World—our last stop before Amtrak in the early afternoon. A delightful place, actually. Just the speed for young children.

Best of all was the face-painting. Katie and Aimee pleaded with me and I gave in ("Oh, okay, it is our vacation, and..."). They didn't want to leave Circus World. There was this little Ferris wheel that they went on about thirty times. Over and again. Round and round. They put up a stink when we had to go. As we drove toward Orlando's Amtrak station, I realized I had absolutely no idea how to clean their faces. I stopped at a rest area on U.S. 4, but soap and water didn't do a thing. It wouldn't be healthy for two kids to travel twenty-four hours on a train with this white and colored stuff on their faces? Would it? I mean, they were professionally done as clown-faces. I drove back to Circus World and re-entered. ("No, I didn't change my mind! We'll be here just for a moment.") At the face-painting tent, they told me the magic word: "Vaseline!" It worked like a charm.

On the train ride back up north, I realized that I had been missing Emily very much.

* za za za*

I do not want to get married again. But it isn't because of Chrissie. You do get to know someone well after almost ten years of marriage, and I knew that Chrissie's message to me was: "Be happy. If you want to remarry, then do it."

Even so, I don't want to get so close to someone and lose her. I do realize that what happened to us was like lightning striking. There's no "curse" or jinx here. I just want a little more time to be *sure of it.*

za za za

In retrospect: When I met Emily, I had already moved through a lot of the grief, although I didn't realize it at the time. It wasn't difficult for me to talk about the accident; it wasn't difficult to talk about my feelings. In addition, I had accepted the idea that Aimee, Katie, and I were already a new "mini-family," not the "bitter fragment" it had felt like for the first two years after the crash.

Most of all, I had not yet met someone (like Emily) with whom I felt totally comfortable sharing these still-very-sensitive feelings. So, it was a combination of two things: One, I had progressed to a certain healthy point (but didn't fully realize it), and, two, I had met the right person. Emily was someone I would have been drawn to even if I had never before been married.

I had dated women after Chrissie died. Nonetheless, when I met Emily I felt vulnerable, for I had no preconceived notion of my "ideal woman." Since I had already grown to understand that Chrissie was not replaceable, I had ceased searching for her. And although I had loved her, I had never had an "ideal" woman, even when I knew Chrissie. Because of this, I met Emily innocently, without having any pre-set agenda for what and whom she should be.

What I just said is probably the most important point about remarriage I can make in this book: I did not reach a place in recovery where I said or felt, "Now it's time to remarry," and hung out a sign, "Open for Remarriage." No. What happened was that when I met Emily I was not only not open to the idea of remarriage, I specifically did not want—or need—to remarry. I had come to a point of comfort with my life. I was earning my doctoral degree, I was getting exercise, losing weight, and so on. Katie and Aimee were doing well in school. They had gotten even closer to me, and close as well to Aunt Ann, Uncle Frank, and Grandma DiGiulio. They did not need a new mother.

It was only *after* meeting Emily that the idea of remarriage grew. It started out by my wanting to be with her, enjoying talking to her, going places with her and even trying to play racquetball with her (fiasco!).

Who is Emily? I wanted to know. And the more I knew, the more I liked her. Loved her. The more I loved her, the less vulnerable I felt.

I had no standards by which I measured Emily. This made it much easier for Emily, who needed reassurance that she was not "taking Chrissie's place" in my life or the lives of the children. I did not compare her to Chris. I never confused her with Chris. And I was "Bob" to Emily, not the ghost of some other guy she once had known.

ら・ら・ら・

Emily (in retrospect):

"The first time I went with you to your house in Vermont I was nervous and excited—this place you had talked about; the house where you and Chris lived with your children. I was nervous about what I might see. I was curious, but afraid to see many signs of Chris in your house. When I walked in, I saw a picture of Chris on the desk in the living room. It looked like a college portrait, with every hair in place. I instantly became very worried about staying over—I didn't want to stay, especially since I'd be sleeping downstairs in the living room, which I realized was full of pictures of her. (As it turned out, I slept with Chris's eyes in a picture looking right at me! What must she be thinking?!).

I knew I loved you and loved being with you, but I was afraid to think of marriage. You would very often say to me, 'I don't think I want to get married again... I don't know if I ever want to get married again...,' and I would think to myself, well, I'll be happy knowing Bob and being together. I'll try not to worry about the future, but I did try to get a commitment from you. Remember? When we were at Hardee's, I used to ask you 'Where do we stand?' 'Where do I stand with you?'"

ɜɜɜ

I really do love Emily, and have decided to ask her to marry me. I made up this letter not to Emily, but to Chrissie:

Dear Chrissie:
I want to get married again. I didn't want to wait and then write you a "Dear-Chrissie-I-got-remarried" letter! You know I loved you when you were here and we were together. I tried very hard to make you happy. But people will now ask, "Remarriage? What about his love for his first wife?"

Chrissie, do I still love you? Yes and no. Yes, I still love the person I once knew; the one now in my memory. But Chrissie, you aren't here anymore. I can't say "I love you," because there is no "you," but in my memory. I can cherish a thought, but I can't love it. I can cherish your necklace, our wedding photos, your deodorant, but I can't love them. I'm a person and I can only love another person. I love your/our children, whom you left for me to raise. Do I miss you? Yes. Do I wish I could see you again? Of course. But I miss my father, too. And I wish I could see him again, too. Someday, I too will be gone, and someone will wish they could see me. But the "right now" is all I have. You are not here now. It is my "now," not yours. It is also Emily's "now."

If you were here I would introduce you to Emily. (I can't tell her this because it would sound quite patronizing, but you'd really like her—she's attractive, kind, and intelligent. She has class.) Emily has a special type of strength that I admire. Her laughter is wonderful, and she looks at me in a very loving way. You know, Chrissie, I do love her. She is very special to me. One more thing: She is very affectionate to Aimee and Katie. In fact, she treats them kindly, very much as you did. And they like her, although they do not see her as the authority figure you were! And they will not be altogether happy sharing me with a stepmother! I do miss you, and I miss your mom and dad. And I miss our little Christine more than anyone—even you— could ever suspect. Please keep her warm. And please love her as only you can. I will love Katie and Aimee as only I now can.

***

What had been keeping me from thinking about getting remarried was my feeling that I didn't—ever, ever, EVER— want to lose someone again. I simply did not want to get close to someone, only to lose her suddenly. Plus, there was no one I wanted to marry.

But being able to spend time with Emily gradually reassured me. What happened to me three years ago was like being struck by lightning. It had nothing to do with me—with my being jinxed. Besides, Emily told me that she felt it was okay if we didn't marry. She told me she loved me and enjoyed being with me, and that was more important than pressuring marriage upon us.

When they first learned about the impending marriage, Katie and Aimee were fairly reserved about the whole idea. They really liked my "girlfriend" Emily, but were unsure what this would mean to their lives. But I didn't push acceptance by either Emily or Katie and Aimee. Time would bring us all closer.

Since January I have spent much time interviewing widowed women and men for my doctoral research project. You would think that they would want to be left alone, but almost every widowed person I contacted agreed to be interviewed. For some people, it was the only social contact they had.

Others saw me as an expert, and a few tried to set me up with a new wife. (I declined, but secretly I loved the attention.)

Interviewing all these widowed people was therapeutic for me. I met one widow whose interview made me laugh all the way back to my apartment. I had to pull into the rest area on the interstate because tears were rolling from my eyes.

One of the interview questions concerned dating— something like "Do you think you would date again?" When I asked this of a seventy-two-year-old New Haven widow, who was a dead ringer for "Whistler's Mother," she eyed me as if I had just landed from Venus.

"Of course I would! As a matter of fact," (she gleefully held up her index finger), "I had my first date last Saturday—he was eighty years old!" She leaned over and joked, "I like older men!"

I asked her how that first date went.

Her brow furrowed. She looked a little tense. Uh-oh. I shouldn't have deviated from the interview format. "You know, you don't have to answer..."

"No, I don't mind the question. It's just that my experience was kind of frightening. You know what I mean?"

I nodded yes, because I knew how odd it can feel holding someone who is not your spouse. Although I knew the answer, I asked, "What do you think made it feel so bad?"

"Well, as we were sitting there, I had to shake him and then slap him."

Ah, feisty old cuss.

"He got fresh on the first date?" I chuckled.

Again, she looked at me as if I were a Venusian.

"Fresh? Hell no! I thought he was DEAD! He was only sleeping, but what a perfectly quiet sleeper! My husband used to snore to beat the band, so I got scared. That's why I slapped him!"

As I drove back that night all I could think of was this wrinkly, dear little old lady shaking and slapping some unfortunate gent sleeping in a movie theater.

Some of my interviews made me feel as if Stephen King had written the script.

In a small town on the Rhode Island seacoast, I interviewed a widow whose house was right on the Long Island Sound. Once I parked my car it took about a half-hour to find her house; brilliant me decided to traipse along the beach, well-lit by a full moon. There are, I soon found out, packs of dogs on this beach at night. Wild dogs. Like flocks of birds, they ran one way, then suddenly changed course and ran the other way. I decided I would play dead if they came near me.

When I got there, the widow opened a huge wooden door and let me into her darkened house. I followed her to a room at the center of the house. She invited me to sit in a velveteen, high-back chair placed in the center of the heavily wood-paneled room. There was one light on—a small spotlight right over my head. I could barely see her shape as she sat across from me against the wall. She lit a candle on the sideboard to her right. Above her head the full moon peered through the window. Then she turned to me, silent. Nervously, I proceeded with my first interview question:

"Many people say being a widow is difficult. How has it been difficult for you?"

She was silent for a moment, then responded:

"That is my husband's favorite chair you are sitting in."

The hair on the back of my neck stood; I peed—but only a little—in my pants. I told her I forgot my stove was left on. I flew out of her house, ran two non-beach blocks to my car, and drove along U.S. Route 1 to the first McDonald's I saw. There I drank coffee next to a group of loud, belching, shirtless urchins with ponytails, wearing sunglasses and sleeveless, studded jeans jackets. I felt safe.

Then there was the one about the funny widow in Springfield, Massachusetts. When I called to set up our interview, she told me she had a rich variety of... widow jokes. (I suppose widow jokes are to be expected. After all, there are doctor jokes told by doctors, teacher jokes told by teachers, and lawyer jokes told by everyone else, so naturally, there had to be widow jokes told by widows.)

Her first one was awful:

"Did you hear about the widowed man who saw the doctor, and told him 'Doctor, my wife died, and I'm afraid now that I will die, too.' I will do whatever you say so I can live.' The doctor said, 'First of all, stop smoking. You must go on a diet and lose weight. Cut out everything alcoholic, and staying out late and running around with women is bad for you.' The widowed man asked the doctor, 'So you say I'll live longer if I do all these things?' The doctor answered, 'No, but it will SEEM a lot longer!'"

She laughed. I cringed.

On Tuesday she called with another widower-doctor joke:

"A handsome and much-pursued elderly widowed man went to see his doctor. The physician checked him from head to toe and said, 'I can't find a thing wrong with you. But,' he cautioned, 'you're not a young man." I suggest you give up some of your love life.' The widower thought about it and asked, 'Doctor, which part do you recommend I give up—thinking about it or talking about it?'"

When I finally interviewed her a week later, she asked if I would be interested in a friend of hers.

"Is this another joke?" I asked.

"No. No joke at all. My friend is really pretty, she's about your age, and has a fantastic personality." Hmmm. I remembered my blind dates with "a great personality."

"Is she widowed?"

"Yes, and she has the sweetest children—all daughters—you'd ever want to see! Your two daughters would get along just fine with all of them!"

"All of them?" I cautiously asked, "How many daughters does she have?"

"Seven. But the oldest is away at college."

Piece of cake. We'd have a baseball team.

Some of my interviews were warm. One Canadian widow talked about the idea of accepting death, and we wondered whether people can ever truly accept the death of a loved one. She told me a story she had heard years earlier and asked me to pass it on to another person, someone who could not yet understand why their loved one had died. It went like this:

Gotami was a poor peasant woman. Neither her family nor her husband's family was very kind, and even when she gave birth to a strong and healthy boy, she continued to be seen by them with disrespect.

Shortly after his first birthday, however, her boy fell ill and soon died. Overcome with grief, she carried his body throughout the village, knocking on doors and asking for powerful medicine to make her son well again. But people only laughed at her, telling her no medicine could bring a dead boy back to life.

By and by, Gotami met a woman who felt sorry for her. She told Gotami where to find the Wise One, who could surely help her. Still carrying her son's body, Gotami went to the land of the Wise One. The holy man greeted her gently, and after Gotami pleaded for medicine for her beloved son, he told her to go into the town. He told her to get a mustard seed, a seed from a family who had not known death and bereavement. Encouraged and full of hope, Gotami set out with her son for the town.

At the first house she visited Gotami asked for a mustard seed. As she was given the seed, she remembered to ask, "Has anyone died in this house?"

"Yes," she was told. With that, Gotami refused the mustard seed.

She went on to another house and as the owner went to fetch a mustard seed, Gotami called to him, "Has anyone in this house known death or bereavement?" When the owner answered "Yes," Gotami again refused the seed and moved on. As she went from house to house, Gotami soon realized that no house had been spared the pain of death. Thus strengthened,

Gotami left the town and carried her son to the burial grounds. There she met others who were separating for the last time from their loved ones. As her son's body was placed on the pyre, Gotami cried deeply but not bitterly, for in her tears she said, "I know now, dear son, that you are not the only one whose death has pained the breast of a mother."

I—like Gotami—realized I was not the only one who had lost someone beloved. I knew, too, that after three and a half years I had finally moved beyond the worst of my loss.

≈≈≈

Emily. It is tough for her. She doesn't admit it, but I know she feels a little funny dating me. We have friends visit; they are my friends, but they were "our" friends—Chrissie's and my friends.
Emily wonders if they are comparing her to Chris.
Are they?
I try to reassure Em:
"No, they're not."
Sure they are.

≈≈≈

In late December Emily and I were married in a simple ceremony at a small country church. Katie and Aimee were our two young attendants, joined by our friends Anne, Neil, and Paul. In fact, it went so well, we married again the following June— a huge outdoor wedding in New Jersey with all our relatives and friends. And the temperature that day exceeded 100 degrees.

1984

Our local elementary school is going through some difficult times. They keep losing staff, especially in the upper grades. Most notably, grades 7 and 8. These rambunctious older kids do not belong in an elementary school to begin with. Trying to get a teacher to handle them has been a chore, especially at the low rate of pay. Fortunately, the town has voted to send 7th and 8th grades to the local junior high school next year. But now, in March, two teachers have already quit teaching the upper grades. The principal asked me to step in to teach the 8th grade—just to get them to graduate in June.

I said yes, I would do it. I made several rules very clear to the students. Rules about respect, and how to address me and each other. My experience teaching in the inner city schools of New York has taught me to keep things very simple, very focused, and very consistent.

With kids in crisis situations, whether it's physical abuse or drug addiction, one of the cardinal rules is to change their environment, and do so as soon as possible. Because I felt these kids were "at risk," I sought and received permission from all the students' parents to take them out of school. Every day. With the mild weather coming, there was so much learning that could take place out of doors. Sometimes, and always on cold or rainy days, we went to my house. I had a huge office, converted from an attached barn. There the students took turns using my computer, operating the word processor. Others typed reports, while another group worked around my desk on a research report I had assigned them. It was a calm and quiet environment, different from the tumultuous, catcall-filled day they had known in school. Sometimes I'd play guitar, and students would learn a new song. Without younger students around, many lost their teenage inhibitions about singing, or speaking out.

At my "home-school," my students did a variety of things— pitching a tent, categorizing wildflowers they found in the nearby fields, measuring the number of seeds needed for my garden, playing wiffle ball. Previously, recess time at school had been hell—with students chasing each other, students screaming at each other, teachers screaming at students for disrupting others' games of jump-rope or kickball.

In May, Emily and I graduated from the University of Connecticut. I received my doctoral degree and she, her masters in education.

In June, the elementary school asked me—"Dr. D"—to be the commencement speaker at the eighth-grade graduation ceremony. I was flattered by the invitation. (Apparently, my students had gotten together to petition for this.) Although I had known these students for only four months, I was so proud of them as they went on stage—the last ever 8th grade at Reading Elementary School. After I gave a brief commencement speech, Emily played the flute, and I, the piano. The students and I felt that "Bridge Over Troubled Water" by Simon and Garfunkel seemed to symbolize their year in school. So we played it, and a piece by Mozart.

These months have been my noblest achievement as a school teacher!

Retrospective anecdote: Throughout that summer, Katie kept referring to herself as "Dr. D's daughter." At first I didn't mind, but Katie kept it up for a year until, late in 1985, Emily finally told Katie she could call herself "Katie DiGiulio."

On the first day of second grade, Katie and I were standing in the midst of a group of parents. One said to Katie, "You're Dr. D's daughter, aren't you?"

"I used to think I was," said Katie, "but then my mother told me that I really wasn't."

ುಲ.ುಲ.ುಲ

1985

In August, my Barbados roommate, Rita, called to tell me she and her Charles DeGaulle–look-alike, Luis, were still deeply in love and had decided to get married. She apologized for not being able to invite Emily and me to her wedding. She explained how her new husband should never hear about "Roberta and Rita" and her/our Barbados escapade.

"He would think we do dilly-dally all night on the boat," she said, "and would be suspicious for me for always."

She added, "We do a lot of dilly, but no too much dally!"

In October our daughter Angela Cara was born. Emily needed an unexpected, emergency Cesarean section, but at least I was allowed to be there—right there. Lucky me! My feelings hovered between fear and terror, but I put up a brave front for Emily: Yes, I'd be, uh, happy to be with her in the, uh, operating room. (My reasons for never pursuing medical school came down to four words: the sight of blood.) Unable (and unwilling) to watch, thanks to a merciful screen placed around her, I held Emily's hand as I locked my gaze on the medics' faces, anxious to detect any sign of the unusual or trouble. Suddenly, the nurse and doctor broke the spell, chuckling "There she is! A gorgeous girl! Staring right at us!" He lifted her and within a moment, placed her in my arms. Unlike my other children born "normally," Angela was clean, large, and unbumpy. Perfectly fluffy, like a Cabbage Patch doll.

In the waiting room, seven-year-old Katie and ten-year-old Aimee were ecstatic, pleading to see (and hold) their new baby sister. Emily and I brought them around to the nursery window, where Angela soon appeared. They smiled proudly, spiritually bonding with their new sister.

I remembered my family—I'd promised to call them all with the news. I raced down the hospital corridor to the telephone, and as I rounded the corner, I stopped short.

I realized that I was back in Springfield Hospital.

Springfield Hospital.

The doors. Those were the same stainless steel swinging doors the police had brought me through five years ago. The same white walls. White tile floor.

This corridor was the very corridor I had run through, a sick, shaking, nervous wreck desperately seeking proof his baby child was alive.

And now, at this moment, my life was two images held up to the light.

There I was then, and here I am now.

But the real shock this time was instantly knowing how far I had come in the five-year circle that brought me back to the doors. I would use the phone this time not to incoherently recount to my distraught family who had not survived the accident, but to tell them what a proud father I had again become.

At that jarring moment, I knew the most severe pain of my loss had departed sometime in the five-year circle, and that here was a new, whole, and very different person now standing in Springfield Hospital's corridor.

1986

Early in spring, I decided to run for the position of Probate Court Judge for Windsor County. Vermont was perhaps the only state that allowed non-lawyers to hold the position. With the primary race set for September, I chose to run as a Democrat. (As it turned out, that was a fatal error.) People who encouraged me to run said that, by my running as an Independent (my preference), I could not enter the September primary, and thus would get almost no exposure between now and the November election. Anyway, I stood outside the local Grand Union supermarket on U.S. Route 4, asking people to sign my petition to get on the ballot. (This practice of going right to the public is common in Vermont—you'll often meet legislators-to-be soliciting signatures outside of the local post office, stores, and near the Town Hall.)

As my campaign got underway, I gradually realized that, even in Vermont, things weren't as simple as declaring your candidacy, winning the primary and becoming the candidate of the party. When I naively attended a Democratic Party meeting (my first) to give a presentation on my position, I was greeted politely, but ignored by the party leaders. I could tell that the probate judge candidate they favored—"their woman"—had already been picked long before I gave my speech. I was "an unknown," and they were determined to keep it that way. While the "designee" was surrounded by a group of laughing people holding drinks, people would come up to me and say, "Now, what was your name again?"

Anyway, my "team" (Emily and two friends and I) forged on. We sent this press release to the newspapers:

Upper Valley resident Robert C. DiGiulio has announced his candidacy for Probate Judge of Hartford District in Windsor County. Presently working as an educational consultant, Dr. DiGiulio has written for numerous magazines and newspapers on the subject of family, and has authored two books, *When You Are a Single Parent* and *Effective Parenting*. The latter book has now been released in Spanish translation.

Formerly a widower, and having been through the process of probate in Vermont, DiGiulio has expressed a strong belief that the Probate Judge should be not only capable, but compassionate as well. "People pass through the Probate process at difficult times in their lives—whether they're widowed or they're young children in need of a guardian. The Probate Judge must be someone responsive not only to the letter of the law, but aware of the disruption of the family that is taking place."

Dr. DiGiulio has served as Principal at Bridgewater and Windsor elementary schools, and has taught at Pomfret and Reading. He has lectured extensively on the subjects of widowhood and single parenting, and in 1985 he guided the establishment of the first self-help group for widowed persons in southern Vermont. DiGiulio is now remarried and resides in Taftsville with his wife Emily and three children.

Dr. DiGiulio, the only non-attorney on the Democratic slate, has two masters degrees, and recently earned his Doctor of Philosophy degree in Family Relations from the University of Connecticut in May of 1984, which included studying Family Law at the University of Connecticut's School of Law. He is a member of the American Psychological

Association, and the National Council on Family Relations.

Compassion almost worked. I finished second in the four-person Democratic primary, but at least had the satisfaction of not only beating two lawyers, but also of receiving the most votes in towns I had worked in and was known: Woodstock, Bridgewater, Pomfret, and three neighboring towns. But the winner easily took the two largest towns in the county, where she had worked for many years as a lawyer. As for me, they say a candidate has to lose at least one election or else it's a bad omen. I'm all set to start my winning streak.

In between working and running for probate judge, I was continuing my "Widowhood Project," organizing research findings for my book *Beyond Widowhood*. The project's purpose was to identify recovery factors in widowed persons. Why did women who had friends adapt better? Why did men generally do poorly unless they remarried? I tried to get funding for my research from the Guggenheim Foundation, Ford Foundation, Catherine MacArthur Foundation, all to no avail. Despite the fact that there were thirty million widowed men and women in the U.S., it just wasn't a hot topic.

I funded it on my own out of my earnings as a college professor. Because I could not continue doing a major research project, I decided to continue to reach out to widowed persons, and maybe even have fun doing it. For example, I wrote a letter to Corazon Aquino, then-president of the Philippines (and a recently widowed woman), asking her if I might interview her by telephone. She never responded. Perhaps she never even got my letter. Maybe I should have called?

I tried to interview Steven McAuliffe, who was leading Senator Biden's campaign to become a presidential candidate. Mr. McAuliffe was an attorney and widowed spouse of astronaut/teacher Christa McAuliffe, who had lost her life in the Challenger space shuttle explosion. I called McAuliffe's law office in Concord, New Hampshire, but he never returned my calls. Maybe I should have written?

Later, in 1989, I learned that Marilyn Quayle—the then vice-president's wife—was interested in disasters and human survivorship. So I wrote her and sent her a copy of my book *Beyond Widowhood*. Perhaps she would read it and give me some feedback or get me a grant to do more research.

Upon hearing this, my brother Tommy reminded me about the Dan Quayle jokes: "If President Bush gets shot, the Secret

Service has orders to shoot Dan Quayle," and Tommy worried that the Secret Service or CIA or whomever might come knocking on my door. They would not take kindly to my sending the Vice-President's wife a book about moving past widowhood!

But to my surprise, Mrs. Quayle wrote back to me—a personal letter—relating how she had witnessed her mother's experience as a widow, and how important she thought my book was. Already impressed by her caring, I was deeply touched by her sincerity.

¿a.¿a.¿a.

In December of 1988, Matthew Christopher DiGiulio was born. We sat for our first family portrait in the hospital, all dressed in white gowns: Katie, Angela, Dad, and Mom with a proud big sister Aimee holding Matthew. We felt whole.

As I drove in my car back from the hospital, I thought about the low value placed upon children in our society. About how each of us is trying to make it in a world that is often hard and uncaring. People are good; it is our system that regards children as property that is defective.

Look at our divorce process, guardianship hearings, and custody battles: Judges are in just about the worst position to decide who should take care of a child, and under what circumstances that child is to be raised. The evidence lawyers present in court is highly biased, designed not to enlighten but to produce victory for one side. This is because our legal system is adversarial: Your side must not only prove the merits of its position, but must also discredit and attack the other side, even when that "side" is your children's mother or father. It is in this adversarial attacking that the seeds of anger and revenge are sown, lingering long past the judge's decree. Family matters of disagreement—divorce, guardianship, custody, estates— should be immediately removed from our legal system and placed in a new, non-adversarial mediation process.

Seeking advice on a real estate matter, I recently sat in a lawyer's office. The telephone rang. The lawyer turned away from me and thundered into the phone:

"Look, I've told you. If he doesn't pay, he doesn't get to see the children."

I looked down at the floor, embarrassed. He threw out his arm. "I don't care how long they've been crying. He didn't think about the consequences when he didn't come up with the payments, did he? You're letting him off the hook if you give in. This is all his fault, not yours!"

He slammed down the phone and looked at me. He shook his head sadly.

"Some people," he said, nodding toward the telephone, "just never learn. I think they actually like to get stepped on..." He was interrupted again by the phone.

"Look," he said, making eye contact with me, "I told you: If he don't pay, he don't get to see the kids."

He held the receiver away from his ear. I could hear her sobbing voice.

"Well, that's *your* decision. You'll *never* get a penny out of him this way. But *that's your decision*," he spoke his last three words slowly and with emphasis.

He slammed down the phone, and looked at me.

"I'm terribly sorry for the interruption. Now, where were we?"

Years ago, people needing help called upon a minister, priest, or rabbi, or an older member of the family. Today we call a lawyer, and we are poorer for it. Poorer emotionally, spiritually, and financially, because we have moved from *social* supports to *legal* supports. But ironically, it is the social supports that are far more valuable. Indeed, after interviewing and examining the recovery of hundreds of widowed women and men, I can state that the single most important factor in whether a widowed person will survive widowhood is not how many rights she has or how much money she possesses, but whether she has a close *friend*. The key aspect to survival is *social,* not political, legal, or financial. Yet more and more emphasis seems to be placed today on the latter.

Men must come to value women's values. It is not impossible. My parents supported many "feminine" values within our family, and I see how crucial they were to my survival: values like sharing ("Share with your brother and sister") and caring (perhaps the greatest offense that could occur in my family was ignoring the needs of a family member). My parents expected respect, and gave respect to each of us.

And instead of pushing women to abandon pro-social roles and careers, we must support men who move into these pro-social roles. Believing that men have female sides as women have male sides, psychoanalyst Carl Jung urged men to get in touch with their female side. To do so, men must relearn many of their patterns of behaving, and women must have the courage to define success in a new way, for what men have called "success" has also brought men stress ulcers, alienation, and aloneness..

This takes courage. The courage to buck society—if you love teaching kids, teach. Whether you're a man or a woman, if you don't want to spend six days a week, fifty weeks a year in a boring, repetitious job, don't do it. If you'd rather work as a newspaper editor than as an advertising executive, go for it. If you'd rather spend time with your family, do it. Live on less money. Go with your kids to the playground, to the library, to the park. They charge no admission. Bring your own lunch. But don't sacrifice what's important to your life merely for the ability to acquire—and then spend—lots of money for what society tells you to value. No man (or woman) on his deathbed ever said, "I wish I had spent more time at the office."

꒰ꓸꓸ꒱

In late 1989 my book *Beyond Widowhood* came out, and I enjoyed a measure of celebrity. Invited to New York to appear on "CBS—This Morning" with Kathleen Sullivan and Harry Smith, my name was mispronounced by Ms. Sullivan. Twice. But I enjoyed undying fame in my colleagues' eyes, since Dolly Parton was the other featured guest that morning. CBS Television sent a stretch limo to pick me up from the swank Hotel Essex overlooking Central Park at 7:00 a.m., and this is true: In the limo there were Bloody Marys, vodka, screwdrivers— the works. Are there really people who can drink that stuff at 7:00 a.m.?

Next came the local and national TV shows and radio talk shows. A big one was "Sally Jessy Raphael" in November. What a class act it was! No quick shuffle or phony scripts. (Sally invited Katie and Aimee to be with me on the set, but during the taping and as she introduced them in the audience and invited them to join me, they slunk down in their seats, petrified.) Sally talked with me before taping the show. She seemed genuinely interested in learning about widowhood, and asked me to feel free to say what I felt—even to correct her if needed. And this is true: She smelled great.

And while it is also true that I was relishing all the attention given my new book (and me), I didn't think it was excessive. However, my brother Tommy thought that with each TV appearance I was becoming more self-centered and insufferable.

After my appearance on Sally Jessy Raphael's show, our dear Mama DiGiulio proudly and predictably told the entire family, her letter carrier, her internist, and every senior citizen she could find in Connecticut about her famous son Bob. *"Dr. Robert DiGiulio."*

A week before my show was scheduled to air, Tommy called me to tell me that my show was going to be on tomorrow morning.

Tomorrow morning? I was mystified. Yes, he insisted, it was so, adding, "Check *TV Guide* if you don't believe me." After we hung up I looked in *TV Guide* and realized his little jest. The subject of "my show" was "The Messiah Complex: Men Who Think They Are Jesus Christ."

Score: Thomas 1; Robert 0.

≈≈≈

In May of 1990 Katie and I were sitting in the family room watching "Jeopardy!"

I noticed she looked serious; she had been deep in thought and seemed to be sad.

"Dad, someday can you tell me about my mom? My real mom?"

After we talked, Katie and I decided to go to Connecticut to go through many of Chrissie's things. Things I had put away eight and nine years ago in my mother's closets. Katie and I pulled down the boxes. Although there were many things that brought back poignant memories (like cards and letters Chrissie and I had written to each other), much of the other stuff looked like somebody else's things.

Now that Katie is becoming a teen, she and Aimee wonder who that woman was who gave birth to them and loved them so much. Ten years after the crash, Aimee's and Katie's bereavement work is not done. They keep a lot inside. They avoid crying; avoid expressing feelings of sadness. They have not yet been able to fully face the "monster in the closet." Whenever the monster makes noise, they run, afraid to open the door and face him.

It is a start for them as teenagers to have things that were Chrissie's. Things that, by themselves won't make the monster easy to face, but will bring them to confront some of the pain they feel. And more than ever, we must talk. I must listen.

This year, I gave them things that were Chrissie's. Katie has

Chrissie's wooden jewelry box; Aimee has her necklace. Both have many pictures; since they were young I have given them their own photos to place in their own albums, albums filled with pictures of everyone, including cats whose names are long forgotten.

Several times we have gone back to the cemetery, where Katie and I planted Chrissie's favorite daisies and wild violets.

The stones still stand there. They help me see how far I've moved, yet they still exert a hold on me—as full as my life is, a part of me is buried there. Not all of me, just a part.

Later that month I was asked to be the commencement speaker at my daughter's elementary school. No, I could not really talk about widowhood and bereavement, not at a graduation! Instead, I decided to share with them a story of my past career as an elementary teacher and principal:

> Thank you for asking me to be your commencement speaker. I want to talk today about what is on the mind of each person here: How can I be successful in the seventh grade?
>
> The first rule is this: You have to show up.
>
> Once upon a time, my Mom went to awaken her son Bobby.
>
> "Bobby, get up! It's late!"
>
> "Oh, Ma! I don't wanna go to school."
>
> But Mom insisted: "Bobby! You have to get up—wash, dress, eat and go to school!
>
> "But I don't wanna go to school!"
>
> "Bobby, what's gotten into you? Why don't you want to go to school?"
>
> "I hate school!" he said. "The teachers hate me. The kids call me names. They make fun of me. They laugh behind my back..."
>
> "Bobby, stop this at once. You—must—go—to—school!"
>
> "Why? Tell me why I hafta."
>
> "For two good reasons: First, you're forty-one years old, and second, you're the principal."

> Whenever people speak at a graduation, they like to talk about how the new graduates will change the world. Very shortly you will be going into the seventh grade.

Have you ever thought about changing the world?

It does still need a lot of changing. Take world hunger. Think about this: if you shrunk the world down to the size of this room, to one hundred people, do you know how many of those people would be hungry? Fifty of the people in this room would be hungry right now. Half of all the people in the world are hungry. Do you know how many of the people would be unable to read or write? Seventy of the one hundred people would be illiterate—unable to read or write. Seven out of every ten people cannot read or write.

So today, while you thank your parents and teachers and everyone at the school for helping you learn to read and write, do not ever forget that there are other people who live very different lives from yours.

All of you will soon have a perfect chance to change the world: You will graduate high school in the year 1996, and most of you will graduate college in June of 2000—exactly ten years from today.

You will be starting your careers right at the beginning of the 21st century—in the year 2000. How exciting. Our world is getting smaller, and by the year 2000, you will have a wonderful chance to help make this world a better place.

As I stand here today, I want to think of one word— the best possible word—that you can carry over the next 10 years, and into the 21st Century. I know the word in my head, but let me tell you about how it got there.

When I was a teacher in New York City, (sixth grade) I taught in schools where the children were very poor. Many parents did not speak English; some parents could not read or write at all.

In September 1975, I was scheduled to teach the 5th grade that was supposed to be the toughest class in the school. Almost every child had repeated a grade. Most had repeated a grade twice.

There was one particularly tough kid who had had a tough time in the fifth grade. And the fourth grade. And the third grade. The first day of school, Vito walked in with a big grin and said, "Hi, Mr. D-I Giulio. I'm the one you heard all about."

I said, "I'm the mean teacher you heard all about."

He said, "You ain't mean." He told me how he "couldn't do no math, couldn't do no reading." I asked him what he could do.

He said he liked music. Vito hated schoolwork, but he really got into it when we had music. I bought 35 black plastic songflutes for my class, and twice a week I'd give them lessons. Vito loved it.

I went home and thought about this tough class. I talked tough, but I felt bad for them, because I had a good life, and wanted them to have a good life too.

How could I help these kids?

The next day we talked about rules for our class: Even though the world was terrible and unfair, we had to survive. If we were going to change it, we would have to start here. Right here. Right now.

We discussed a plan for the classroom, and Vito was the one who came up with the word:

(LOUDLY) "Mr. DiGiulio, the problem with these kids is that they got no respect for nobody cause nobody got no respect for us."

We talked more, but agreed that there was one word that would guide us through the year. A code word.

Our word was "respect." Respect every other person in the class. If a boy was giving an answer to a question, and someone was trying to make fun of him, that would not be respectful.

This included property, too. When a pencil fell on the floor, there was no need to fight over who owned it—right? Wrong. If someone dropped a pencil on the floor, Vito would say, "Uh-no. Finders-keepers, Man. Finders-keepers." "But Vito," I'd ask, "is that respect?"

Most important was simply, "Respect yourself." If you did well on a test, it was okay to feel good about this achievement. If you did not, you still had to respect yourself: Your failure on one measly test did not make you one bit less a good person. My little friend, Vito, tried hard but failed about half the tests in the sixth grade. His written homework was even less impressive.

Six years after Vito left my sixth-grade classroom, I
ran into his mother and found out he had made first
clarinet in the New York City All-city Orchestra,
composed of the best musicians from all the New York
City high schools. As a teacher, I like to think that I
helped give him a start. But he was the one that made
good things happen, by respecting others, and by
respecting himself.

As you go into the seventh grade, I want to wish you
good luck. Good luck. But there is much more to success
than luck: Respect other people and their things, and
respect yourselves. The world will quickly and clearly
tell you the things that you do not do well. But each of
you has something good that you can do, even if it
isn't *the best* in the whole wide world.

Remember that we are all very fortunate to live in
this country, especially today with much of the world
in turmoil.

You know, I spoke to a group of preschool children
last year and told all the little children what a wonderful
country this is. I told them why I thought so:

"Because everyone in our country is free."

A little preschooler stood up and said,

"Not me," he shook his head. "I'm four."

Have a wonderful summer, and make good things
happen in the seventh grade!

ta.ta.ta

In April of 1991 we began weekly family therapy. For Emily
and I saw signs that worried us; signs that should concern any
parent of any adolescent, even one who has not experienced
Katie's and Aimee's losses: I saw feelings not being expressed,
disregard for school work, long and unaccounted-for time spent
in the privacy of a bedroom, temper tantrums, unexplained
absences from home, and sadness. After ten years, the monster
is still in the closet.

Have I failed? As I look back over the ten-plus years since
the crash, I know that my daughters' fully dealing with their
losses is not something that is accomplished easily or quickly
or after a defined period of time. I am sad to say this, but one
year, three years, even ten years are not enough time to heal
the loss of a loving mother and sister and grandparents. Maybe
they will never fully accept their deaths, but they have to—at

the very least—heal their hurt. It is one thing to look back on the pain and feel sad, but another matter entirely to walk around still wounded and hurting.

Although I have personally and privately relived my life with Chris and my dear baby Christine so many, many times since their deaths, and have moved beyond the pain and loneliness of their loss, I realize it has been different for Katie and Aimee, who know little of Chrissie and Christine. I am healed; they are not fully healed. Before Aimee and Katie can truly get on with their own lives as adults, they need to first "get to know" Chrissie. And then they need to face the monster in the closet. To say goodbye to their mother.

It is time to open the museum once again, for their sake.

I take a deep breath and sit down, for after ten years of working through so much, my real work as their surviving parent is only now beginning.

But they have, perhaps intentionally, already helped me to now be able to help them. Because they once needed me so desperately, I simply had to start living for *them*—the living— and less and less for the dead. Now it is time to help them live for themselves.

As we trudged across the grassy knoll in the Vermont cemetery ten years ago on the day four beloved ones were buried, I held Katie in my left arm and Aimee walked beside me holding my right hand. With four fresh graves behind us, I said nothing as we approached our car. As we neared the car, I realized—for the first time —that it would carry only three of us back home.

As if she could read my mind, Aimee looked up at me just before we reached the car and broke my terrified silence:

"You know Dad, you still got us!"

And that moment became the pivotal moment of my life: I made a conscious and firm resolution *to survive*. If only for their sake, I would survive and I would flourish.

It's my job now to return the favor.

PART FOUR: LOOKING BACK

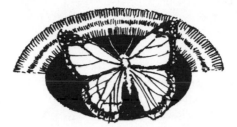

If life must not be taken too seriously
then so neither must death.
—Samuel Butler, "Death", 1912

Loss is the most emotionally painful of all human experiences. And the varieties of human loss are many: Women have miscarriages. Loved ones die. People experience divorce. They lose their jobs; they go bankrupt; they are convicted of a crime or fall ill to a disease. The greatest pain from any loss—divorce, widowhood, death of a parent, child, or even a pet—comes from its ability to force us to face our solitude, our *alone-ness* in the world. (If I have one striking recollection of my most immediate feeling upon first hearing that my wife had died—even before numbness and denial set in—it was a terrifying sense of aloneness—of being vulnerable; of being *all by myself* in the world.)

The good news is that our facing this aloneness is necessary: It will become the key in our design to go on living, the linchpin in our survival. For no matter what the cause of our loss, survival requires that we face our aloneness, and survival demands that we do so constructively. Or else we live lives of recurring grief, filled with regret, anger, sadness, and pain.

"Facing our loss" sounds fuzzy; impossible to define. As we ask what it means to "face our loss," we must remember that survival is nothing more than *learning*. There is not one divorced man or woman alive who has not learned something very important about marriage. Even in the animal kingdom, survival comes to those who learn, and quick demise comes to those who cannot. For humans, this learning involves—in the face of loss—learning what to do, what to say; whom to be with; where to go; how to continue to live. The learning must be practical.

Because I have moved beyond painful losses in my life, people regard me as a "survivor." I have learned much from my experiences. Accordingly, they tend to ask me questions like, "What helped you move on? What was most helpful? Not helpful?" Another, second type of question I am asked, usually by a family member or friend of a hurting person, is "How can I help someone who has experienced loss? What can I say; what can or should I do to help?"

As I look back and scrutinize Year One of my aloneness—those eternally long days, weeks, and months right after the crash—I see matters that can and should be emphasized. In retrospect, certain things I learned were extremely important in helping me survive. On the other hand, I can also see a number of things that proved to be not helpful. Let me start with the "first-year unhelpfuls":

What did not help me: Valium. It slowed me down, made me lethargic, and did not promote my recovery. Why do they prescribe sedatives for bereaved people?! Perhaps it helps not so much the affected individual but those persons around him or her. It is, after all, they who are thus comforted, gazing comfortably upon not a tearful, crying human being, but a zombied lummox.

I do understand, however, why it was initially prescribed for me. When they brought me to the hospital, it was either give this guy Valium or hit him with a sledgehammer! I raised hysteria to the level of fine art that day. Valium was the immediate treatment of choice for my irrational hysteria. But not after it subsided (within a few hours). Not after the first day. I erroneously thought that Valium would continue to provide a mellow feeling, and I renewed my prescription for the first three months, taking Valium when I felt especially anxious. Yes, it eased my anxiety, but although I fell asleep fairly quickly, I would awaken feeling both grief-stricken *and* dulled.

Alcohol did not really help, either. Actually, I drank little, because I did not enter bereavement as an alcohol-liking person. And I never drank when I had taken Valium (thank goodness!). But the two times I really drank—at a friend's July 4 cookout and on that first New Year's Eve without Chrissie—I simply got giddy, then felt miserable, then fell asleep. The worse part was that both times I awoke with a pounding headache. The hangover made it worse. Please believe me: Alcohol—drinking—is a very bad idea after loss.

Although I participated in (and was asked to speak at) self-help and support group meetings, it would have helped if I had involved my daughters and myself in a community religious or spiritual group. Perhaps even a nonconventional one.

We tried to attend conventional churches early on, but I felt uncomfortable with much of it. For example, it was difficult for me to hear well-meaning but strange explanations offered Aimee: "God wanted your Mom." "God wants all good people." "God has a plan for everything." So I tried to provide my family with spiritual guidance on my own, drawing much strength and support from our close friends in the community, and from my larger family, even though they were miles away in Connecticut and New York City.

I have always marveled at how family-oriented many of my Jewish friends are. Jewish spirituality seems centered inside the home and within the fabric of family, including extended family. While I came from a close, loving, Italian family that had Catholic holiday traditions at Easter, Lent, and Christmas, we had to go outside our home—to Church—for our spiritual matters. And the sacraments and the Mass didn't come into our homes, so I grew to see little connection between home and religion.

I quit my job. That was not helpful. Although I had a small outside source of income, it was not quite enough to keep us going. Thus, after six months I began to sponge off my family. Eventually, one has to re-enter the job market. Therefore, it is better to do so sooner rather than later, because it is much more difficult to jump back in the water downstream. (This is precisely the career-versus-home dilemma women have faced for years.)

Furthermore, do not switch jobs within the first year. If you like your job, working at it will protect you from a number of the bad effects of loss. Employment allows you to remain productively occupied, and it provides an already-in-place support system.

What is also helpful after loss? Sex helps. As I look back, it was difficult for me to write about sex in my journal. Nonetheless it was a part of my life then, and is a reality all hurting people must face. Learn about safe sex. This is especially important for people who have been married and monogamous. If having sex outside of marriage would violate your religious beliefs or make you feel uncomfortable, decide whether the guilty and/or sinful feelings you may experience are worth it at this time.

Don't confuse sex and love and marriage. Especially love and marriage. Some people mix them all up even under normal circumstances, but people who are hurting are not in any position to commit themselves—emotionally and/or legally— to another person. Make believe there is a law prohibiting you from remarrying until FOUR years have passed. (Okay, THREE years, but not a day less.) Before three years, commit yourself to another person as a close friend—exclusivity is fine. You might even fall in love with him or her. You may consequently choose to become intimate (have sex), but do not do so if you believe that one must then make a legal commitment (get married) as a result of being sexually involved. Contrary to the old song, love and marriage *do not* go together after loss. Research has shown that marriages made within the first year of bereavement may be the shakiest and most likely-to-end-in-divorce of all marriages! Marriages made by newly-divorced persons are also shaky. If your friend insists on marrying but three years have not passed since your (or his/her) spouse has died, or your (or his/her) divorce, tell him or her to wait.

As I look back, I can see what contributed greatly to my initial pain after loss: My anger at the incompleteness of Chrissie's life. She was stopped, literally, dead in her tracks. That left me, again literally, with a houseful of unfinished business. From the most basic (her freshly laundered underclothes still in the dryer) to the significant (her children and husband needing her love), Chrissie's death left many remainders—reminders of the suddenness of her departure. What helped me greatly was learning how to (gradually) finish her business. At the very beginning, I did the most mundane things: I folded her laundry and put it on top of the dryer. I weeded the violet bed she favored. Because I still smoked cigarettes then, I finished off her half-carton of Parliaments when I ran out of my brand, using "her" ashtray near "her" side of the kitchen table. I sat at her seat at dinner; slept on her side of the bed at night. I did housework the way she had done it—cans go here, milk goes on that side of the refrigerator door, frying pans stacked at the bottom under saucepans.

Eventually, I got into more of her personal things: She had been working on a latch-hook rug; I pulled it out of the canvas bag and finished it. I used her body powder; I used her underarm deodorant.

Learning how to do, and then actually doing, all these things helped in many ways: It made me feel closer to her. It helped me to deny that she was gone (very important early on). It made the starkness of her departure more gradual—I could make things not appear to have been sharply broken off. And it helped Katie and Aimee by keeping their routines both intact and familiar.

By finishing Chrissie's unfinished business, I—ironically—came to know her even better after death, for only then did I take on part of her persona; I became whom she had been. We were legally "one" in marriage, but were truly, spiritually "one" only after she died. While this sounds falsely romantic, it did happen. My handwriting resembled hers. I heard myself speak her pet phrases. Gradually, I incorporated who she was into who I was. But also gradually, I did go my own way (our own way?), partly due to weariness and partly due to necessity. I stopped smoking, I put the milk on a more convenient shelf, her/our/my frying pans were now hung over the stove, and I went back to using Mennan Speed Stick. Yet by completing much of Chrissie's unfinished business and by thus incorporating her into my identity, I was ultimately freed to go ahead on my own. Her/our/my.

This is an especially critical point, for it allows a hurting man or woman to move on to a new relationship with a new lover, without being encumbered with the unfinished business of a past relationship. I could not have remarried three years later, or ever, had I not gone through this phase after loss.

Divorced persons can put the past in perspective after their losses. Although our legal system forces divorced persons to become hardened enemies, it helps greatly to bring to mind the good that you once shared, and to keep it alive within yourself in the same her/our/my way. Especially for the benefit of your children.

After loss, people may "look for" their loved one. At the very beginning, I searched for—and was visually drawn to—women who looked like Chrissie, or who had one or more of her physical features. In public I would see a woman facing away from me and I would be secretly mesmerized by the fact that she was Chrissie's exact height, body build, and hair color. When she would turn around, no matter how otherwise attractive she was, her face would be a caricature of Chrissie. In response I'd be disappointed, feeling strangely cheated by a face that did not match. Nevertheless, "searching" for a lost loved one is quite normal, and it is an important part of working through grief. The painful truth is that you will not find him or her. It's just that you need time to realize this. It cannot be rushed.

My very first date (a blind date) came in August, only two months after Chrissie died. (I still can't believe I did it, but my flesh was crying for the touch of a woman... no, it was crying for more than a touch.) A college friend hooked me up with a lovely widowed woman from Rhode Island. We hit it off immediately, spending our first date talking about what we had in common, namely, sharing our stories of That Day. Eventually (later that evening) we became intimate, with the understanding that having sex implied no deeper commitment—we openly agreed that it was too soon for either of us to think clearly. Yet I knew things were over one month later, when she called me "Mike" during lovemaking. She was embarrassed, but I made a joke out of it. (I told her to call me "Big Mike" during sex.) If my being "Mike" made her feel better, I'm glad for it. But that's when I knew that, as fetching as she was, I could never consider making a serious commitment to someone who still needed to see and feel *Mike* in her life. Her career and my returning to work made it difficult for us to keep up our Vermont–Rhode Island connection, so we gradually spent our little time together simply talking on the phone.

Years later, through our mutual friend, I learned that she did eventually remarry, a "dynamite" and caring guy.

And his name really was "Mike."

Thank God.

Family can be very beneficial. Learn how to allow them to help you. I used my sister, Ann, and brother-in-law, Frank, as baby-sitters when I needed to go out, and they did double duty as counselors, drinking decaf coffee with me long into the night when I couldn't sleep and needed to talk. My sister-in-law, Paula, and niece, Andrea, were in that category, talking with me and listening through countless hours on the telephone. What made these people special is not that they were family, but they were my friends. Family-friends.

Aside from family-friends, I had splendid friend-friends. Joseph Matarazzo, former president of the American Psychological Association, spoke about how crucial friends are to our well-being:

"More psychotherapy is accomplished between good friends at coffee every morning at ten o'clock than all day long in doctors' offices. A good talk with a close friend can solve problems, or at least put them in some perspective, before they become overpowering. One of the problems we face today is the scarcity of good friends."

As I look back over my journal, I see that I mentioned friends only in passing. Like air and water, we usually take our good friends for granted. But from the very first day of my pain, I had no lack of good friends. Hurting people talk about how important it is for others to "be there" when they're needed. My neighbors were my friends, and they were there. They would come by and talk and have coffee. Neil and Anne Marinello would visit, and as their daughter Heather played with Katie, we would talk. Anne and Neil helped me work through my feelings of grief, and we did so while enjoying being together as friends.

In addition to being my friend, Neil Marinello also happened to be a skilled psychologist and therapist. Shortly after Chrissie died, Neil and I were riding in my car heading to play racquetball. He asked me what had been good about my marriage. I rattled off a list, and began missing her as I spoke. Then Neil asked me what was not so good about being married to Chrissie. "'Not so good'? There was *nothing* bad about my marriage!" I asserted, irritated to even *consider* such a thing. But by suggesting I question my "perfect marriage," Neil helped me begin to see my relationship with Chrissie with some objectivity. Looking back now I see that this was a turning point: I began to allow myself to think "the unthinkable." As Neil and I rode to racquetball, Chrissie was perfect, our marriage had been ideal, and nothing would ever be right again. After that evening I had a more objective view; our marriage *had* been... well, yes, less than perfect. Although I didn't understand it at the time, this realization opened me to the possibility that I could love another someday. If my past had stayed "perfect," nothing—no one else—could ever match that ideal. Neil helped me immensely. I repaid him by winning our racquetball match.

Becoming close to people is the single most helpful

investment you can make in your becoming whole again after loss.

What else was helpful? As I look back, I see that *activity* was crucial. In two ways: One, it gave me something to do with my otherwise unstructured leisure time, and two, it gave me hope, something to look forward to. One of my most vivid memories as a child was sitting outside on a sweltering New York City night in July awaiting the arrival of the Good Humor ice cream truck! The first faint, far away sound of the truck's bells stirred such excitement within me, and it grew as the sound got louder. The anticipation was even better than the ice cream. Although Good Humor ice cream trucks' bells are long gone, there are other "bells" for us as adults.

The only problem is that we have to actively make them happen.

We can't demand the luxury of sitting back and awaiting them as we could do as children. For example, although it was costly, my Barbados cruise gave me pleasure, not only from the experience, but also just looking forward to it! Truly, my cruise was the highlight of an acutely painful first year.

As far as raising my children goes, I do not have any great regrets. Like most parents, I believe I have become wiser with age. If I had it to do again, I would have been more "dictatorial," especially when it came to their school activities: I would have insisted that they participate more in after-school and summer activities. Like many parents, I gave my children slack—I wanted them to learn to make their own decisions, so I allowed them to choose much of the time. But I overestimated their ability to make good and informed choices at an early age. Finally, I would not permit one of their responses to be "none of the above," or "do I hafta?"

Recent research backs up this idea: In a major study at the University of Chicago, researcher Benjamin Bloom found that parents of successful children all had one thing in common: Without "pushing" their children, these parents made clear their expectations that their children become involved in an interest or activity (piano lessons, skiing, swimming, science, sculpting, etc.) and expected their child to follow through with the activity once begun. Knowing what I know today, I would have been stricter about not letting the girls off so easily. Not feeling like doing something is not good enough. Children who are dealing with loss issues are prone to feelings of depression and low self-worth. Yet allowing them to temporize—to wallow—helps no one.

Remember that for you or for children it is hard to stay depressed when you're actively doing something you enjoy doing. If there's nothing you enjoy doing, it's still better to do what you must do instead of doing nothing.

ᏜᏜᏜ

The second question is, how can I help someone who has experienced loss? What can I say; what can or should I do to help? Being around a person who has suffered loss can be discomforting, and we get little preparation for these situations. Hence, I have developed the following responses to the question, what should I do? not do? what should I say? when a friend has lost a loved one, or has experienced any loss, including divorce or unemployment:

* What to do?

Be there, even if there's nothing to say or do. This is why solitary confinement is considered to be a form of torture by international human rights groups. Human presence is the simple but most powerful antidote to aloneness. This presence is especially important in the period right after the loss. Support drops off for hurting persons after a few weeks: "She's back together"; "She's her old self—why, she looks great!"

Make yourself available, not inevitable. Offer to mind children, do housework, care for pets, or just sit and cry or watch TV together.

Listen. Just listen. Shhh. Listen. Look at the person. And as you listen, accept his or her feelings. This may be hard to do, because we wish the person's hurt to go away. Remember that there are no bad feelings, only happy, scared, mad and sad ones, and each needs to be expressed without being evaluated.

Above all, respect the person's need for dignity. In our winning-is-everything society, loss (divorce, death, and so on) places adults in a socially weakened, inferior position. Don't try to force a hurting person to move in the "right direction." One culprit insisted, "My mother needs to face reality." "Whose reality?" I asked. "Hers? Or yours?"

Encourage physical activity. People who said to me, "Let's take a walk—how about some exercise?" were helpful. Activity is beneficial.

Encourage self-reliance, too. Do not leap to do something

that a hurting person can do for herself. Be wary of "relieving" a hurting person by, for example, insisting on minding her store, her children or her pets; these "burdens" might otherwise give her early days meaning and activity. Remember that recovering from loss—any loss—lies in learning new ideas, skills, and attitudes to fit the new situation. There will be disappointments, false starts, and backsliding.

* What to say?

Say, "I know how you feel," only if you truly do. Better than saying it, show it by being there and listening. And show it by your actions. Hurting persons can be disturbed by insensitive behavior that, under other circumstances, may be harmless. For example, a widowed woman told me how angry she still was at her sister-in-law's loudly voiced concern for which outfit would look best to wear to the funeral.

Bluntness can be risky. Never confuse being honest with being blunt. When honesty is not tempered by good judgment, it is bluntness: Telling a divorced woman, "You're better off without him," may be accurate, but is also distressing. Telling a widower, "Your wife never had this house looking so clean," or telling a widow, "Bill did have a bad drinking problem," may be precise observations, but they can be disturbing and serve no constructive purpose.

It doesn't help to share too much unsolicited information and advice all at once. Sharing facts from your similar experience may be helpful ("I also lost a child..."), but the hurting person's learning must take place over time—over the upcoming days and weeks and months. Remember that you are probably in a more advanced stage of acceptance, and your attitude may appear to be too casual or flippant. Sharing helps, but only later when the hurting person is ready to hear.

Use humor, but sensitively. Clever comments made early on can have a paradoxical effect. Take a cue from the hurting person. Never poke fun at the deceased or ex-spouse, even if others do, or even if it's accurate. What appears to be humor to you may be sarcasm and bitterness, which your endorsement will only magnify.

If you ever simply do not know what to say, simply say nothing. Or say, "I simply don't know what to say."

Talk and act practically. Deeply philosophical ideas are lost on hurting men and women. Offer practical, concrete help: "Does your daughter need a ride to school tomorrow?" "I'm on my way to the supermarket. Do you need anything?" "Can we meet Sunday after church for breakfast?"

How else can I help?

Orient the family toward each other. At an appropriate time, help a teen become cognizant of his hurting mother's needs: "She could use you to be with her." Likewise, hurting adults need to talk about their children, and things close to them. They are worried for their children, and children worry for their parent.

Involve the children where possible. If you will be joining the hurting person for shopping, lunch, or another social outing, consider asking him or her to invite the children, who are sometimes overlooked or unwelcome at these times. Be aware that teens, however, are often hesitant to be seen with a parent, especially under circumstances like divorce or the death of a parent that makes him or her "unusual," different from peers.

What should I watch out for?

Avoid "becoming" the missing parent. Or the ex-spouse, deceased or not. Simply be yourself. Doing "what Ben would have wanted me to do" is a surefire way to stir up deep resentment from Ben's wife and Ben's kids. Your loyalty to Ben is now best shown by being sensitive to those Ben loved.

Unless you're a doctor, don't diagnose. Since physical illness is more common in hurting persons, encourage him or her to see a physician for a checkup. This is a good idea for anyone.

Watch for unusual signs after loss. Get help if you're unsure. If someone's pain seems unusually strong or long-lasting, let the person know he or she does not have to experience this alone. "It looks like you're having a difficult time. I have an idea that may help." Involve a professional, especially if there are any thoughts, indications, or expression of suicide.

Ultimately, the only challenge after loss is in *survival*, and the only means we have to survive involves our *learning* to move beyond loss. After much personal experience living through losses and after professionally interviewing hundreds of bereaved men and women, I can summarize what I have learned over these years into three "musts" for hurting people to survive and thrive: Commit, Let Go, and Connect.

Commit. Commit means to plan, and then to *do*. Commit means to keep occupied with work, to stay on your job. Make a resolution to be active, to exercise. Commit yourself to drug-free living. Give yourself things to look forward to. Get a new pet and care for it. Care for people, too: Volunteer to help others. Take up and carry on with the work of the loved one who has died. Some of the most successful people began by picking up where someone had left off. But if it is work not to your liking, give it up to another and pursue your own line. Return to school; prepare for a new career. Decide to get a checkup from your doctor, and see it through.

Let go. If commit means "to move toward," "let go" means "to leave behind and move away from." Letting go allows creative change into your life. Move away from the pain, hurt, insults, and rejections of your past. Free yourself to express your sadness, but let go at least a little of it each time. Express your happiness, because letting go means laughing, too. But most of all, letting go means accepting that loss and death are a part of life. Once you accept the fact of death, *let go of all thoughts of it, for it is impossible to live your life and at the same time dwell on death.*

Connect. With at least one other human being. Isolation and loneliness are killers, especially of hurting people. Join or rejoin a religious group. Pray/meditate/contemplate. Be part of a singing group. See yourself healed and whole. Care for yourself. Care for someone else, and let someone care for you. Ultimately, we must begin taking care of each other. More than anything else, our survival as a human race depends on it.